VOLUME 20

FAIRCHILD-REPUBLIC
A/OA-10 WARTHOG

BY DENNIS R. JENKINS

SPECIALTYPRESS
PUBLISHERS AND WHOLESALERS

Published by
Specialty Press Publishers and Wholesalers
11481 Kost Dam Road
North Branch, MN 55056
United States of America
(612) 583-3239

Distributed in the UK and Europe by
Airlife Publishing Ltd.
101 Longden Road
Shrewsbury
SY3 9EB
England

ISBN 1-58007-013-2

Designed by Greg Compton and
Dennis R. Jenkins

Printed in the United States of America

TABLE OF CONTENTS

THE FAIRCHILD-REPUBLIC A-10 THUNDERBOLT II

PREFACE

The Fairchild-Republic A-10A is the only Western fixed-wing aircraft which has been designed without compromise for the close air support (CAS) mission (the Su-25 "Frogfoot" shares a similar design philosophy). All of its unique characteristics originate from CAS requirements, including its low speed, long endurance, extensive armor, and heavy built-in armament. However, its dedication to the unglamorous CAS mission has also been the reason why it has been largely overshadowed by its supersonic contemporaries.

The A-10 was christened "Thunderbolt II" during the delivery ceremony for the 100th aircraft on 3 April 1978, perpetuating a trend for "II's" best represented by McDonnell's very successful Phantom II. The ceremony was suitably grand, and was centered around a display comprising the A-10 and its P-47 namesake.

A cloud of gun gas indicates that the GAU-8 30mm cannon is being fired. (U.S. Air Force)

A somewhat less grand event had taken place at Eglin AFB five years earlier. Discussing the A-10 for the Tactical Air Warfare Center (TAWC) Review, Major Michael G. Major closed his presentation by proposing a name for the new aircraft. Republic's first jet fighter, the F-84, had less-than sparkling take-off performance which earned it the nickname "Groundhog" or simply "Hog." Its swept-wing development, F-84F, became the "Superhog," and the concrete-hungry F-105 was christened "Ultrahog." Taking into full account the general configuration of the A-10, along with its multitude of exterior bumps, Major proposed an appropriate name: "Warthog." However, hating the complexity of a word with two syllables, the crews eventually shortened this to simply "Hog" (usually pronounced "Hawg") . So, despite official efforts to the contrary, the A-10 will most probably be best remembered as the Warthog.

Although the Warthog has developed almost a cult following amongst its fans, it has not been the subject of many books. Those readers who want more excellent photo coverage of the A-10 should pick up a copy of Don Logan's *Republic's A-10 Thunderbolt II: A Pictorial History*, which will probably remain the ultimate photographic work on the A-10 for the foreseeable future. Don was kind enough to allow me access to his vast photo collection for this book. And Warthog fan Ken Neubeck has produced two works for Squadron Signal, the most recent being an entry in the *Walk-Around* series due to be published sometime in 1999. Ken is a former reliability engineer on the A-10 program, and contributed greatly to this publication also. Readers interested in a fascinating account of the A-10's role in the Gulf War are encouraged to read William Smallwood's book, *Warthog*.

Another note of thanks goes to Doug Nelson at the Air Force Flight Test Center Museum at Edwards AFB. Anybody interested in the history of modern military aviation should support this museum by becoming a member. Write them at AFFTC Museum, 95 ABW/MU, 1100 Kinchloe, Edwards AFB, California 93524-1850 or call (805) 277-8050. Doug kindly provided me access to the sole YA-10B, even though the aircraft is not currently on display.

This book would not have been possible without a great deal of assistance from a variety of individuals. Mick Roth, as always, provided terrific assistance in locating data and images. Tony Landis had the dubious distinction of providing photographs twice, courtesy of the Post Office losing the original package. Many thanks to SSgt. Gina Farrell at the 422nd FW/PA for the great cover photo. And many thanks to my mother, Mrs. Mary E. Jenkins, who always inspired me to write, and who continues to provide critical encouragement.

CLOSE AIR SUPPORT

The close air support (CAS) mission is probably the least understood in military aviation. It is usually defined as the use of air power to attack hostile ground forces which are already in contact with friendly troops. This definition, however, is not universally accepted, nor adhered to. The amount and type of air power available for this mission varies greatly, and the importance of the mission is hotly debated within the world's air forces. The friendly troops want a lot of accurate firepower, and they want it immediately since it frequently means the difference between life and death. Most ground commanders would like to think of close air support as an extension of their own artillery support—available when and where they want it, without waiting or asking permission from higher authorities. Along these lines the former Soviet Union believed that close air support should be provided by the ground forces' organic assets, mainly helicopters; a view generally shared by the U.S. Army and Marine Corps. In actuality, the CAS controversy is only truly applicable to the U.S. and the former Soviet Union since few other countries have the resources to dedicate aircraft to the role.

Ignoring the political implications of giving ground forces control of their own air support, the basic controversy over CAS aircraft is nearly half a century old: is the role best handled by a specialized type, or by a fighter equipped with bomb racks? The fighter-jocks point to the success the fighters enjoyed in the CAS role during World War II. Advocates of the specialized CAS type argue, with some justification, that the modern "fast-mover" fighter is ill-equipped to perform the mission since its high fuel consumption and poor low-speed handling tend to confine it to a single run against a previously well identified target.

During World War II the Luftwaffe's primary close support weapon was the Ju-87 dive-bomber, which was highly effective during the early stages of the war, even though by most measures it was already obsolete. The RAF and the U.S. Army Air Force had ordered dive-bombers similar in concept, but they did not lend themselves well to Allied tactics, and very few of them were used in their intended role. Instead, the most successful Allied close support aircraft were Typhoons, Tempests, P-51 Mustangs, and P-47 Thunderbolts—fighters armed with heavy guns and unguided rockets. Although not ideal, the fighters proved very capable in the role.

The memories of the 1944–45 campaign were still fresh when the Tactical Air Command (TAC) was formed in 1947, and when the independent U.S. Air Force followed later that year. One of the first directives issued by the Air Force abolished the "Attack" category from its designation system. The multipurpose fighter-bomber became the backbone of TAC, a category also expected to perform the close support role. In the post-Hiroshima environment, the importance placed, and the funding available, to a military organization was

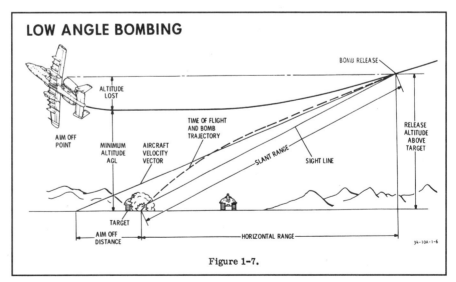

LOW ANGLE BOMBING

Figure 1-7.

There are three main weapons in the A-10's inventory—the 30mm Avenger cannon, AGM-65 Maverick missiles, and a variety of "iron" bombs. Most bomb deliveries are made from low altitude in low angle attacks, frequently exposing the A-10 to hostile ground fire. (U.S. Air Force)

By 1993 the A-10 had received its last major external modifications—formation light strips, new antennas, and fairings over the gun cooling vents on the forward fuselage. (David F. Brown via the Mick Roth Collection)

directly related to its ability to perform a nuclear mission. TAC's major new project for the 1950s was a fighter-bomber designed to fly at near-supersonic speed at low level, navigate to a known ground target in bad weather, and deliver a nuclear bomb from an internal weapons bay. This aircraft was the Republic F-105 Thunderchief.

The F-105 typified a great many trends in fighter design. It was much larger and more complex than its predecessors, and cost a great deal more to acquire and maintain. The F-105 could operate only from well-equipped bases, and although its range was excellent at high cruising speeds, its endurance, in hours, was poor. The F-105 simply could not respond to a call for immediate support from ground troops, nor was it intended to. Nevertheless, the "Thud" would eventually win great respect during Vietnam, dropping iron bombs it was

never supposed to carry, in a war it was not designed to fight.

By 1960, TAC's less sophisticated fighter-bomber types (F-84, F-100, etc.) were getting old. Instead of planning a direct replacement, TAC was working on SOR-183, a requirement which defined an aircraft even larger and more sophisticated than the F-105. Nobody appreciated the implications of this trend more clearly than the U.S. Army, and in 1961 the Army began to seriously consider acquiring its own CAS aircraft. Both the Northrop N-156F (which had not yet received its first Air Force order as the F-5) and the Fiat G.91 were evaluated, along with an unusual British aircraft called the Hawker Kestrel, which later became the AV-8 Harrier. This began a bitter interservice dispute over the division of missions between the Air Force and Army. Finally, the Army had to accept tight restrictions on the

types of fixed-wing aircraft it could operate, but the Air Force was ordered by Defense Secretary Robert McNamara to rebuild its ability to provide battlefield air support.

Not wanting to divert any serious resources from its newfound nuclear strike role, the revival of close support within TAC was originally a very limited effort directed at defeating guerrilla forces in an unsophisticated air environment. Air superiority was assumed, and the resulting "Counter-Insurgency" (COIN) philosophy called for delivering small weapon loads against guerrillas located near friendly forces. In the late 1950s North American Aviation had developed a strengthened, re-engined adaptation of surplus T-28A trainers for the French forces in Algeria, and the Air Force began to procure the similar T-28D for use by indigenous forces and the rapidly growing con-

tingent of U.S. advisors in Vietnam. Various modifications of the venerable P-51 Mustang were also evaluated, although the P-51 had never been a favorite for the close support mission where its belly-mounted radiator proved exceptionally vulnerable to ground fire. The first practical application of the new counter-insurgency concept came in South Vietnam, where the Air Force's first COIN detachments arrived in late 1961. They did not fare particularly well.

Without altering the underlying COIN philosophy, the Air Force drafted a requirement for a replacement aircraft of about the same power, payload, and speed of the T-28D. The aircraft was to be armed with fixed 20mm cannon, and be able to carry a variety of unguided rockets and light bombs. Interestingly, the ability to carry paratroopers was included in the specifica-

tion. The proposed Light Armed Reconnaissance Aircraft (LARA) was to be built in large numbers for the Air Force, Navy, and Marine Corps, as well as for U.S. allies. North American Rockwell eventually won the LARA competition with the OV-10 Bronco.

The Viet Cong, however, refused to cooperate and began to demonstrate a disturbing proficiency with their Soviet-supplied anti-aircraft artillery (AAA). Losses of T-28Ds mounted steadily in 1963–64, and TAC's COIN experts attributed them mainly to the type's modest speed and lack of armor, limitations largely shared by the LARA. Even before the OV-10 made its first flight, TAC had decided that it would be confined to the forward air control (FAC) mission, and by late 1964 there were beginning to be references to a faster, more heavily armed, Super-COIN aircraft.

The need to replace the increasingly vulnerable T-28D was becoming ever more urgent, and the situation became worse in early 1964 when the Vietnam-based Douglas B-26s were grounded by structural problems. Fortunately, a temporary replacement was available in the Navy's Douglas A-1 Skyraider. The A-1 was not fast, but it was reasonably tough, maneuverable at low speeds, and had a long endurance with a heavy weapons load.

The A-1, called the "Spad" by most, proved by far to be the most successful CAS improvisation in Vietnam, and one even shot down a MiG-17 which strayed in front of its four 20mm cannon. It was a decisive participant in many rescue operations, mainly because it could remain on station long after the sophisticated fighter-bombers had turned for home, out of fuel and ammunition. In the CAS mission,

The large trailing edge flaps contribute to a slow landing speed to aid in short field operations. Originally the flaps could extend up to 40°, later restricted to 30° on the preproduction aircraft, and finally to 20° on operational aircraft. The false canopy on the fuselage bottom is noteworthy. (Michael Grove via the Mick Roth Collection)

After Desert Storm, the A-10 fleet began receiving a two-tone grey paint scheme to replace the dark European One scheme used during the Gulf War. The new grey scheme is different than the original MASK 10A scheme. This aircraft has not received the night vision modifications. (Ben Knowles via the Mick Roth Collection)

the A-1's endurance allowed it to loiter just behind the battle area and quickly respond to calls for support from ground troops. Its low-speed maneuverability, and the all-round visibility from its bubble canopy allowed its pilot to see and attack targets that a jet pilot would miss. A small turning radius allowed the A-1 to maneuver and turn among hills and low clouds, in conditions where jets were confined to a single relatively high-speed pass at the target.

The Air Force also used other aircraft for the CAS mission during Vietnam, mainly the F-100 and A-37, but none had the A-I's endurance, so they had to be kept on the ground until needed. Often they arrived too late, or found the tactical situation had changed, and their pilots could not locate targets quickly enough to attack on a single pass. Experience showed that a second pass was frequently fatal to the attacking pilot. Vietnam convinced the Air Force that a highly maneuverable, long-endurance aircraft, relying primarily on the "Mark

Although the A-10 fleet was not completely retired, over 180 aircraft were nevertheless sent to AMARC at Davis-Monthan and put into flyable storage. This aircraft still wears its Desert Storm nose art. (Bob Shane via the Mick Roth Collection)

One Eyeball" for target acquisition, was the most effective way to provide close air support.

Meanwhile, the increasing strength and sophistication of the Viet Cong was not living up to the early-1960s image of a "limited war." Radar-directed AAA was encountered over Laos in 1964, and soon spread elsewhere in Southeast Asia. To make matters worse, regular North Vietnamese Army forces were encountered in the Ia Drang Valley during late 1965 and the possibility of encountering hostile armor could no longer be ruled out. It was becoming evident that any Super-COIN aircraft would have to be able to destroy heavier targets, and survive against more sophisticated defenses, than had been envisioned a few years earlier.

The Super-COIN aircraft was expected to have a simple but

strong airframe, a large weapons load, great resistance to battle damage, and excellent low speed agility. Some analyst in the Pentagon determined that during a war in Europe there would generally be 4,000 feet of runway left in operation after an anti-airfield strike. This distance was therefore written into the requirements as the maximum ground roll for a fully armed aircraft. A lightly loaded aircraft would need only 1,000 feet. The new aircraft was also to be designed to survive in the "... anticipated ground fire environment of the 1970s and 1980s," which suggested a great deal of armor protection and systems redundancy.

But the U.S. Army was not convinced it could rely on the Air Force, and began development of the Advanced Aerial Fire Support System (AAFSS) during 1964. The non-specific program title masked the

WARBIRD**TECH**
SERIES

fact that AAFSS was to be a 254 mph all-weather strike aircraft, although technically it was a compound helicopter. While the Air Force would have produced a CAS aircraft in any case, the timing and details were certainly influenced by the pressure from Army aviators.

Another piece of the puzzle fell into place during 1966, when the Air Force ordered the Vought (LTV) A-7D Corsair II strike aircraft. The Corsair was about the same size as the Skyraider, but had a longer range, higher operating speeds, and much more sophisticated equipment. Its presence in the TAC inventory would help fight the temptation to upgrade the Super-COIN into another fast, expensive, long-range strike aircraft.

The A-10 was scheduled to be retired in the early 1990s, but Operation Desert Storm changed the Air Force's mind. The aircraft lived up to its designer's promises of being a superb ground attack aircraft and tank buster. (David F. Brown via the Mick Roth Collection)

One of the DT&E aircraft poses with a full load of 500-pound iron bombs. This aircraft had a very unusual paint scheme, appearing variously tan, light green, and grey, depending upon the lighting conditions at the time. The A-10's flight test program was fairly uneventful. (Tom H. Brewer via the Mick Roth Collection)

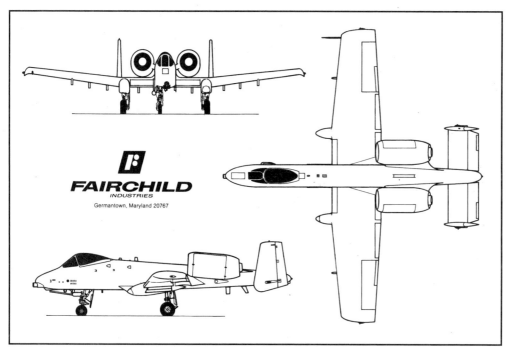

FAIRCHILD
INDUSTRIES
Germantown, Maryland 20767

(opposite page) The A-10 is probably the last American aircraft without fully retractable and covered landing gear. As can be seen here, the main wheels are partially exposed when retracted into the wing sponsons. Note the 2,000 pound bombs on the fuselage stations. (Mick Roth Collection)

(left) The A-10 has one of the most unique external configurations of any modern American combat aircraft. (Fairchild-Republic)

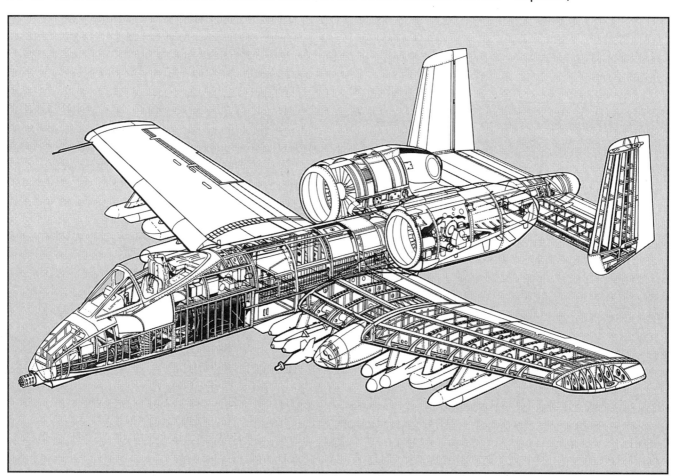

The A-10 has an extremely strong airframe, with three main spars in the wing and horizontal stabilizer. A decision was made to retract the main landing gear into sponsons located under the wings rather than break the wing structure to house wheel wells. The GAU-8/A 30mm cannon and its ammunition drum occupies almost the entire forward fuselage under and behind the cockpit. (Fairchild-Republic)

ATTACK-EXPERIMENTAL

AN OLD PHILOSOPHY FOR A NEW BATTLEFIELD

In mid-1966 Air Force Chief of Staff Gen. John P. McConnell launched the Attack-Experimental (A-X) program by forming a project office at Wright-Patterson AFB, Ohio. This project office was originally responsible for both the A-X and the F-X (F-15), but the F-X was later split out to allow each office to concentrate on their own aircraft.

A request for proposals (RFP) was issued to 21 companies on 6 March 1967, outlining the Air Force's concept for the new aircraft. The RFP was stated in broad terms, listing only the most significant features which had been deemed necessary by the Air Force, and it was not expected to lead immediately to a full-scale development contract.

Ideas and suggestions were solicited from industry in an attempt to define the best possible aircraft for the mission, while keeping within the expected budget limitations.

The A-X was to combine the endurance and weapons load of the A-1 with a minimum speed of 400 mph, a substantial improvement over the A-1's 275 mph with a heavy load. The Air Force wanted a highly maneuverable aircraft which could turn in a limited amount of airspace in order to attack an objective without over flying nearby defenses, or make a complete turn in poor visibility without losing sight of the target or hitting nearby hills. The A-X would also have to be inexpensive, at least compared with supersonic fighters, and be designed to use short, semi-prepared airfields, and to function with the limited maintenance facilities usually found at such bases.

Equipment was to include sufficient armor to protect the pilot and critical systems from heavy-caliber AAA fire. To assist in this effort, study contracts were issued to General Dynamics, Grumman, McDonnell, and Northrop on 2 May 1967 for detailed research on exactly how the armor should be configured and located; how fuel, hydraulics, and other systems should best be protected and routed; and where necessary, what systems should be duplicated. It was reasoned that these large aerospace companies would have the resources and computer modeling

The main and nose landing gear retract forward without turning or folding as with most modern fighters. This is part of the A-10's survivability features since the gear can "fall" down aided by the slipstream if all hydraulics are lost. The only hydraulically-actuated gear door is one covering the nose gear. All other doors are mechanically linked to the gear struts. (Mick Roth)

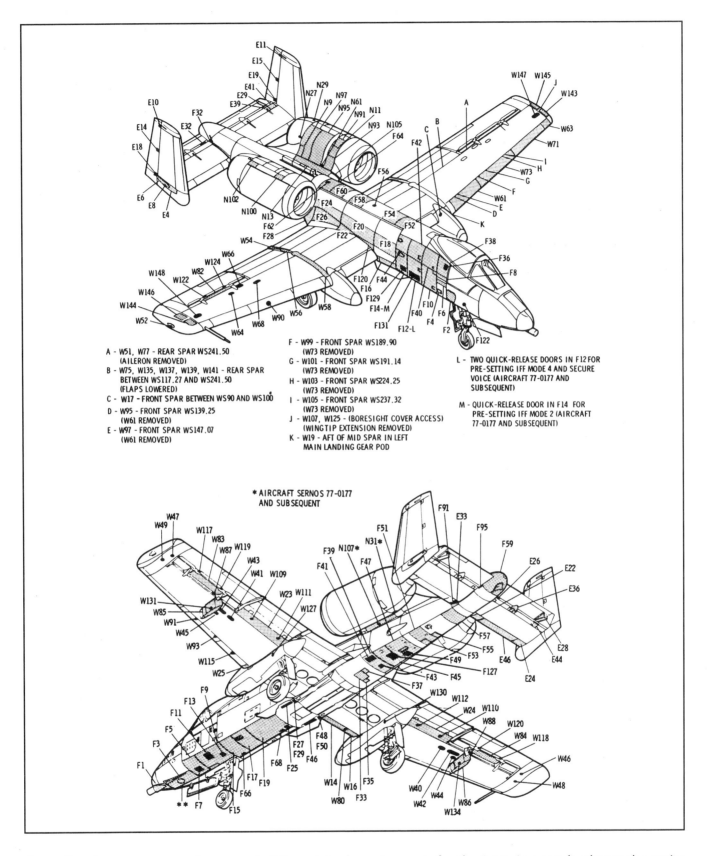

A - W51, W77 - REAR SPAR WS241.50
(AILERON REMOVED)
B - W75, W135, W137, W139, W141 - REAR SPAR
BETWEEN WS117.27 AND WS241.50
(FLAPS LOWERED)
C - W17 - FRONT SPAR BETWEEN WS90 AND WS100
D - W95 - FRONT SPAR WS139.25
(W61 REMOVED)
E - W97 - FRONT SPAR WS147.07
(W61 REMOVED)

F - W99 - FRONT SPAR WS189.90
(W73 REMOVED)
G - W101 - FRONT SPAR WS191.14
(W73 REMOVED)
H - W103 - FRONT SPAR WS224.25
(W73 REMOVED)
I - W105 - FRONT SPAR WS237.32
(W73 REMOVED)
J - W107, W125 - (BORESIGHT COVER ACCESS)
(WINGTIP EXTENSION REMOVED)
K - W19 - AFT OF MID SPAR IN LEFT
MAIN LANDING GEAR POD

L - TWO QUICK-RELEASE DOORS IN F12 FOR
PRE-SETTING IFF MODE 4 AND SECURE
VOICE (AIRCRAFT 77-0177 AND
SUBSEQUENT)

M - QUICK-RELEASE DOOR IN F14 FOR
PRE-SETTING IFF MODE 2 (AIRCRAFT
77-0177 AND SUBSEQUENT)

* AIRCRAFT SERNOS 77-0177
AND SUBSEQUENT

Ease of maintenance was a key aspect of the original requirements for the A-10. As a result, almost the entire exterior surface is covered by access panels and inspection openings. The large openings under the forward fuselage provide access to the General Electric GAU-8/A 30mm cannon, while the openings under the rear fuselage allow access to the auxiliary power unit (APU). (U.S. Air Force)

Two A-10As from the 422nd FW approach a tanker after gunnery practice. Note the amount of black residue on the left side of the forward fuselage of the aircraft on the left. Although all are practice rounds, the weapons load is fairly typical—a single ALQ-131 ECM pod, two AIM-9 Sidewinders, two AGM-65 Mavericks, two LAU-10 rocket pods, and two triple ejector racks with 500-pound bombs. (U.S. Air Force via SSgt Gina Farrell—422nd FW/PA)

techniques to accomplish this research, which would then be made available to all A-X contenders.

Ultimately, the A-X requirements were very different from the updated Skyraider which had been the starting point for the Super-COIN. Most of the initial A-X studies centered around a Canberra-sized aircraft weighing approximately 40,000 pounds and costing $1.5 million each. But one part of the concept still had not fallen into place. With the jet engines available at the time, it would not be possible to match the Skyraider's endurance. The available low-bypass-ratio turbofan engines, such as a Pratt & Whitney TF30 or Rolls-Royce/Allison TF41, had relatively poor efficiency at low speeds. The A-7, which used those engines, had

One of the A-10s from the formation above gives a better view of the weapons carried under the wings. There are a total of 11 stores stations under the wing and fuselage, allowing the A-10 to carry almost any air-to-ground weapon in the U.S. inventory. The location of the in-flight refueling receptacle on the extreme nose shows up well from this angle. The A-10 is one of the few aircraft where the receptacle is immediately ahead of the pilot. (U.S. Air Force via SSgt Gina Farrell—422nd FW/PA)

WARBIRDTECH
SERIES

A-10s were sent to Aviano AB in Italy for Operation Deny Flight. Typically, a "deep" ALQ-131 pod was carried on one outboard wing station while a pair of AIM-9 Sidewinders were carried on the opposing station. (917th WG/PA via Don Logan)

decent range at Mach 0.75–0.80, but burned fuel almost as quickly at half the airspeed, severely limiting its loiter capability. Improving propulsive efficiency at lower speeds meant imparting a lesser acceleration to a larger mass of air, and in 1967 the only established way of accomplishing this used a propeller.

Although they solved the endurance requirements, propellers brought their own problems. The survivability requirements dictated two engines, and the speed and short-takeoff-and-landing (STOL) capability desired by the Air Force demanded large propellers, so the engines would have to be well out from the centerline of the aircraft. It became difficult to design the A-X so that it would be controllable if one engine failed at low speed, especially during takeoff. Northrop looked at the possibility of cou-

As part of 1994's 50th anniversary of the D-Day invasion this A-10 (80-0149) was painted with a set of "invasion stripes" on the wings and engine nacelles similar to those worn by the original Thunderbolts during 1944. (Keith Snyder via Don Logan)

pling two turboprops in the tail, as on the Learfan business aircraft, but this would have made the entire aircraft vulnerable to a hit on the single propeller and gearbox. An alternative used a cross-shaft to interconnect the two engines (as currently used on the V-22), but this added weight and complexity. The overall effect was that the turboprop-powered A-X became steadily larger, with a take-off weight approaching 60,000 pounds, and accordingly more expensive.

Meanwhile, the Air Force continued to refine the A-X requirements in an attempt to minimize the size and cost of the aircraft while ensuring that all the service's essential

needs were met. They also worked on setting up the program structure to avoid the risk of delays and cost escalation. The Air Force was already in political trouble over two major programs, the F-111 and the C-5, and had no desire to add A-X to the list. Moreover, while cost increases could be grudgingly tolerated for an advanced technology aircraft, they would be disastrous for A-X, which was billed as a low-cost, low-risk concept.

Unrelated events were driving the A-X to take on even greater importance in Air Force planning. Disturbed by the lackluster performance of its F-4s against MiG-17s and MiG-21s over Vietnam, and by

the sudden emergence of the Mach 3-capable MiG-25 Foxbat, the Air Force had decided that the advanced F-X fighter program should be optimized for air-to-air combat. In fact, the F-X soon adopted a "... not a pound for air-to-ground ..." motto. From 1968–69 onwards, the entire Air Force CAS mission was riding on the A-X. If aircraft did not materialize, the Army would demand and get all the funding it wanted for the AAFSS,

which had now materialized as the ambitious, sophisticated, expensive, and ultimately unworkable, Lockheed AH-56A Cheyenne.

Another significant change of emphasis began to occur during 1967–68. The North Vietnamese Army had made their first use of tanks against U.S. forces, and conventional warfare in Europe was once again being considered likely. The anti-armor capability of A-X

began to take on considerably more importance. During the 1967 war, the Israeli Air Force had succeeded in knocking out a large number of tanks with the 30mm cannon fitted to their Dassault Mysteres, proving that while considerable advances had been made in frontal armor since 1945, tanks remained vulnerable from the rear, sides, and top. Various tests and analyses had shown that the very successful 20mm General Electric M61, although a superb air-to-air weapon, simply did not have the punch to knock out even moderately armored ground targets. Therefore the A-X would be designed around a high muzzle velocity 30mm weapon that would be substantially larger than the M61. The A-X was turning from a general-purpose bomb truck into a cannon-armed "tank buster," a breed which had been considered extinct since 1945.

Four years elapsed between the first A-X discussions and the final RFP. By 1969 the target weight had been reduced to 35,000 pounds and the projected cost lowered to $1 million. Studies were beginning to show that a new generation of high-bypass-ratio turbofan engines was likely to be more economical than turboprops, and also offered other advantages. The lack of pro-

This unusual angle gives a good look at the upper fuselage detail of the A-10A. The engines sit just forward and above the horizontal stabilizer, which shields the exhaust from observers on the ground while it cools. Fabric covers are normally stretched over the engine intake and exhaust while the aircraft is on the ground to prevent unwanted debris from entering the engine. (SrA Chris Steffen—422nd FW/PA)

The Ling-Tempo-Vought (LTV) A-7D Corsair II was at various times a saviour and a threat to the A-10. Early in the A-X proposal period the acquisition of A-7s took schedule pressure off the A-X and prevented the A-X from becoming a fast interdiction aircraft, a role the A-7 played well enough. Later, Congress would mandate a fly-off between the A-7 and the prototype A-10 in an attempt to kill the A-10 program and procure additional A-7s. The A-7 also demonstrated the deficiencies associated with its low-bypass ratio turbofan engine when it came to low speed endurance, something the A-10 needed in abundance for the CAS role. (U.S. Air Force)

pellers meant that such engines could be located closer to the aircraft centerline with the attendant reduction of asymmetric handling problems. Turbofans were also easier to install and maintain, with fewer complex components (e.g., propeller and reduction gear). The bypass air also helped reduce the infrared (IR) signature, and the engines were exceptionally quiet. High-bypass turbofans were being tested by all the major engine manufacturers, and although they had been designed for civilian airliners, the technology was proving to be applicable to military uses.

In a major change from the way most military aircraft had been pro-

cured for the previous 20 years, the new Secretary of Defense, Melvin Laird, brought back the concept of "fly-before-buy" by evaluating rival prototypes. Competitive prototype RFPs were released to 12 companies on 7 May 1970, specifying an anticipated program of 600 aircraft at a unit cost of $1.4 million in constant FY70 dollars, with a contingency inflation allowance of 15%. Performance requirements included a speed of 400–460 mph and a maximum take-off distance of 4,000 feet with a 16,000 pound external load. The engine choice was left to industry, but the use of high-bypass-ratio turbofans of 7,000-10,000 pounds-thrust was recommended. Sufficient fuel was

to be provided for a 285 mile radius of action, with a loiter time of two hours, while carrying a warload of 9,500 pounds and 1,350 rounds of ammunition. According to the RFP, the A-X should be sufficiently maneuverable to operate safely and effectively with a 1,000-foot ceiling and 1.15 mile visibility. The RFP noted that "Weather conditions worse than this exist only 15% of the time," although it did not specify to what part of the world this figure applied.

The competitors would also be assessed on other requirements. Survivability, or the ability to survive hits from a range of current and projected Soviet AAA

Very little remains of the Republic advanced V/STOL fighter projects that were made in conjunction with various European countries. This model was found in a small museum at the Amsterdam airport and shows a very unique configuration. Small movable wings that retract flush with the upper surface of a fixed delta wing provide additional lift during low speed flight. Four thrust vectoring nozzles, similar to the Harrier, are under the delta wing. The landing gear configuration is extremely unusual. (Dennis R. Jenkins)

weapons, was the most novel. The Air Force wanted an aircraft which could sustain serious damage and stay airborne. But above all, the A-X was to be a simple aircraft, and was not to use cutting-edge or untried technology, both to reduce costs and to eliminate the possibility of schedule or cost overruns.

Responses were received from Boeing-Vertol, Cessna, Fairchild-Republic, General Dynamics, Lockheed, and Northrop on 10 August 1970. The program was significant since

it was expected to be the last major combat aircraft procurement of the decade. The field of contenders was strong. General Dynamics and Lockheed were among the most capable aerospace companies, but both had black-marks associated with the C-5 and F-111, respectively. Cessna had experience with the T-37 and A-37. Northrop had shown how to build effective combat aircraft with comparatively low purchase and operating costs in the F-5. Boeing Vertol, a helicopter manufacturer, was an unexpected participant, and submitted the only propeller-driven design. Beech, Bell, Grumman, LTV, McDonnell, and North American declined to bid.

The Republic Aviation Division of Fairchild-Hiller had learned a great deal from the performance of its F-105 in combat, but had not produced a new aircraft since. Republic had been involved in two separate efforts to develop advanced supersonic V/STOL fighters in collaboration with European countries, but neither had come to fruition. The company had also been a finalist in the F-X competition, ultimately losing to McDonnell Douglas for the F-15. Of all the A-X contenders, Republic was the only one which risked disappearing as a prime contractor if its bid was not successful.

Simultaneously with the A-X, the Air Force issued an RFP for a 30mm cannon with a rate of fire of 4,000 rounds per minute. This high rate of fire effectively dictated that the new weapon would be a multibarrel Gatling-type. While the caliber was not as large as that of some World War II airborne antitank cannon, the weapon would make up the lost impact energy with an exceptionally high muzzle velocity: 3,500 feet/second, equal to the best 20mm weapons in service and considerably better than most heavy cannon. It should be remembered that the overall size of a gun increases rapidly with greater caliber. The mass of each round rises with the cube of the caliber, and the loads on the breech, barrel, and feed systems follow suit. Barrel length increases with the caliber and the velocity. By the time the RFPs were issued, it was clear that the new cannon would be among the largest weapons ever mounted on an aircraft, eclipsing even the 75mm cannon which had been tried during the 1940s. As in the case of the A-X airframe, the new cannon was to be selected after a competitive prototype evaluation process. General American Transportation, General Electric, Hughes, and Philco-Ford responded to the cannon RFP.

A-10s are designed to operate from austere airfields, requiring a minimum amount of support equipment. Here a squadron of A-10s prepares to fly from Indian Springs near Las Vegas. (Dave Begy via the Mick Roth Collection)

THE FIRST BATTLE

The evaluation of the airframe proposals was quick, and on 18 December 1970 the Air Force announced that Northrop and Fairchild-Republic would each build two A-X prototypes. The new aircraft received their official designations on 1 March 1971: the Northrop YA-9 and Fairchild-Republic YA-10. Northrop's contract for the YA-9 was for $28.9 million while Republic received $41.2 million for the YA-10. The difference in funding was because Republic planned to build an aircraft close to production standards, while Northrop preferred to build a classic prototype which would show what the production aircraft could do, but would not necessarily represent it internally. The prototypes would be armed with the standard M61 20mm cannon while the new GAU-8 was being developed.

The decision on the new cannon was also announced: General Electric and Philco-Ford would build competing prototypes under $12.1 million contracts. The two cannon prototypes would thus cost fully one third as much as the four aircraft. Hughes licensed the Oerlikon 304RF-30 as an "insurance policy" in case the main development effort ran into unexpected problems. On 15 January 1973 the two GAU-8 prototypes began side-by-side ground firing trials at the Armament Development and Test Center at Eglin AFB. Initial tests concerned the accuracy and general functioning of the weapons and proceeded until the required 4,000 rounds per minute was attained. General Electric chose a seven-barrel configuration, while Philco-Ford opted for a six-barrel design. The use of multiple barrels allowed a very high rate of fire without exceeding the temperature limits of the barrels, since each barrel actually fires at a relatively slow rate. The advanced family of ammunition types was tested separately from a single-barrel test stand. General Electric's experience with Gatling-type weapons, and the company-funded research on advanced 30mm weapons which it

The first YA-10 prototype being readied for shipment to Edwards AFB inside a C-124 Globemaster. At this early point it had not been decided to name the A-10 "Thunderbolt II", but the idea was surely in the minds of Republic, hence the banner on the manufacturing plant. Both YA-10 prototypes, and the first YA-10A DT&E aircraft would be airshipped to Edwards for their first flights using the specially built cradles shown here. The wings, engines, and tail surfaces were removed in New York and reassembled at Edwards. (Cradle of Aviation Museum via Ken Neubeck)

By the time the first DT&E aircraft was shipped to Edwards AFB, a Lockheed C-5A transport was available. This meant that the engines did not have to be removed prior to shipment since the aircraft was wide enough to swallow the A-10 with the engines installed. (Cradle of Aviation Museum via Ken Neubeck)

had started in 1968, told heavily in its favor. On 21 June 1973 General Electric was awarded a $23,754,567 firm-fixed-price contract for 11 pre-production GAU-8/As, three for quality testing, and eight for installation in the preproduction A-10s.

By the end of 1970, there were three active CAS programs underway in the United States: the A-X competition; the Army's AH-56A Cheyenne; and the Marine Corps' acquisition of the Hawker Siddeley AV-8A Harrier. Congressional critics,

struggling to fund the Vietnam war, wanted to know why all three types were necessary. To find an answer, the Department of Defense (DoD) began an extensive study of CAS doctrine and tactics in February 1971. About the same time, the Air

The second DT&E aircraft was the first A-10 to fly out of the Republic Airport. Later production aircraft would fly out of the Hagerstown plant since it was determined that the old Republic company airfield, which had been converted to a civilian airport years earlier, was not an appropriate place to conduct flight tests. (Cradle of Aviation Museum via Ken Neubeck)

Force was working on its own study, TAC-85, which covered the entire spectrum of tactical missions. One of the most significant aspects of these studies was that they concentrated on potential wars in Europe as opposed to the ongoing conflict in Vietnam.

The DoD study reached the same conclusion as the ground force commanders already had. The U.S. military simply did not have anything in service which could perform CAS effectively. For the first time the reports referred to the sheer quantities of Soviet armor forces staged against Europe, and to the potency of air defense systems such as the SA-6 surface-to-air missile (SAM) and the ZSU-23 mobile antiaircraft gun system. The DoD tried to explain that the size and sophistication of the potential threat made CAS very complex, and that the three CAS types under development were each specialized to handle a unique part of the mission. The report summarized the usage of the three types: "Cheyenne in discreet, responsible, highly mobile units, operating as part of the ground maneuver force; Harrier in rapid response to urgent firepower requirements during amphibious operations; and A-X in concentrating heavy firepower, matching selected munitions to different targets, at threatened sectors from dispersed bases." It was conceded that the capabilities of the three types might overlap "... in less demanding situations," but concluded that all would be needed to fully counter the expected Soviet threat in Europe.

The Northrop and Republic design

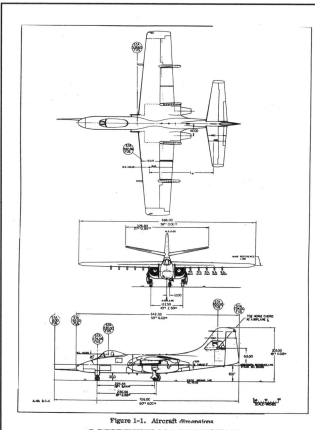

Figure 1-1. Aircraft dimensions

1-2

COMPETITION SENSITIVE

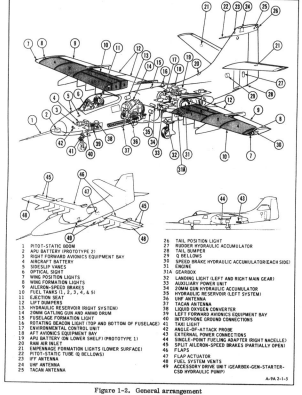

Figure 1-2. General arrangement

1-6

COMPETITION SENSITIVE

The Northrop A-9 was a much more conventional aircraft, at least in appearance. Like the Republic design, it featured a large bubble canopy that provided excellent visibility in all directions. However, unlike the A-10, the A-9's engines were mounted low, under the wing where they might have been vulnerable to ground fire and did not benefit from the exhaust "shielding" provided by the A-10's horizontal and vertical stabilizers. All of the fuel was carried in wing tanks in the outer wing panels. The idea was to keep the fuel well away from ignition sources, such as the engines, but would have made proper armor protection difficult. The "side-force control" system proposed by Northrop did offer advantages during maneuvering during attacking. (Northrop Corporation)

approaches were very different, including their external configurations. The Northrop aircraft followed fairly conventional fighter practices, with a shoulder-mounted wing, single vertical stabilizer, and engines tucked under the wing close to the fuselage; in fact the whole aircraft greatly resembled the original Bell XP-59A. The YA-10, on the other hand, did not resemble any previous combat aircraft. Its engines were mounted high and outboard on the rear fuselage between twin vertical stabilizers, and the main landing gear retract-

ed into sponsons under the wing. It was difficult to fathom how the two aircraft materialized from the same requirements.

Both the Northrop and Republic contenders featured combined aileron/speedbrake surfaces on their outer wings. These resembled conventional ailerons, but were split into upper and lower panels. When opened, they produced a powerful deceleration effect with virtually no trim change, unlike a fighter-type dorsal or ventral speedbrake.

The Northrop Corporation Aircraft Division YA-9 used semimonocoque fuselage with a riveted stressed aluminum alloy skin. The pilot sat in a protective "bathtub" of aluminum armor, although titanium was expected to be used in the production aircraft. A large bubble canopy gave the pilot 360° visibility to provide optimum target observation, and he sat on a zero-zero ejection seat. The YA-9 featured foam-filled fuel tanks in the wings outboard of each nacelle, well away from ignition sources. Redundant hydraulic flight control systems

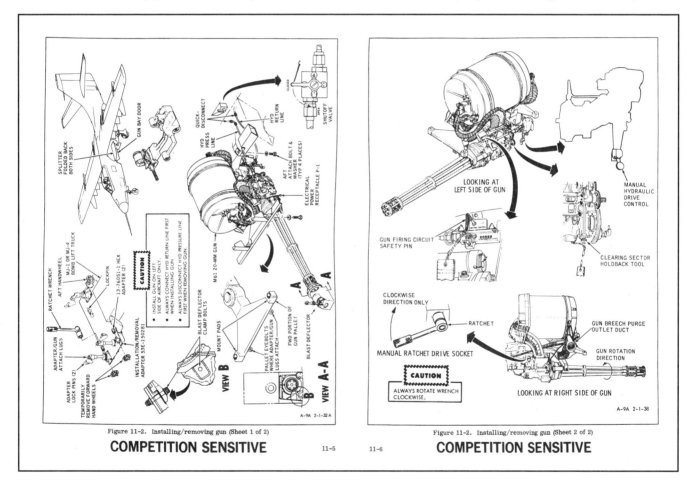

Figure 11-2. Installing/removing gun (Sheet 1 of 2)
COMPETITION SENSITIVE   11-5   11-6   Figure 11-2. Installing/removing gun (Sheet 2 of 2)
COMPETITION SENSITIVE

Like the prototype A-10s, the two YA-9s were armed with General Electric M61A1 20mm Vulcan cannon. The cannon was mounted further aft in the Northrop design, and was self contained on a pallet that could be removed using a standard Air Force bomb truck. Also like the A-10, the cannon was mounted so that the firing barrel was on the aircraft's centerline to minimize the effects of the gun's recoil. Overall the A-9 and A-10 were judged to be roughly equal in terms of performance and capability. The A-9's low wing was considered less ideal since it restricted access to the weapons stations, forcing the ground crews to duck under the wing while securing and arming ordnance. (Northrop Corporation)

The two YA-9s languished at NASA's Dryden Flight Research Center for several years before they were finally relegated to museums. The #1 prototype (in back) went to the Castle AFB museum, while the second aircraft went to March Field. (NASA/DFRC via Tony Landis)

bay, just aft and below the cockpit carried a 20mm M61A1 in the prototypes, but would have housed a pallet-mounted 30mm cannon in production models. Each engine nacelle was structurally integrated into the fuselage and wing, and contained a Lycoming YF102 engine at the aft end, an accessory gearbox, and the main landing gear. An APU and air-conditioning unit were mounted in the fuselage center section.

The 58-foot wing was equipped with ten hard points for external ordnance. Stations 4 and 7 could carry external fuel tanks, but the prototypes were not plumbed for fuel. Fowler-type flaps extended over half the wing trailing edge on both sides of the fuselage. Large spoilers on the upper wing trailing edge assisted in short field landings. The YA-9 also featured a unique side-force control (SFC) system that linked the speedbrakes and the large rudder. SFC was a mechanization of control surfaces to perform azimuth corrections without bank or sideslip. To achieve this, the rudder produced side force in the direction of the turn, while simultaneous asymmetric (left/right) speedbrake deflections negated the yawing moment introduced by the rudder. Control of the asymmetric speedbrake and rudder

provided protection against battle damage and a third cable-operated manual system provided an additional measure of safety in the event both hydraulic systems failed. The GAU-8 cannon would be mounted along the longitudinal centerline of the fuselage to eliminate recoil effects on the yaw axis.

As a result of the cannon's location, the nose landing gear was offset one foot to the left of the centerline.

The nose section housed electrical and avionics equipment, sideslip sensors, the nose landing gear, and liquid oxygen equipment. The gun

When Castle AFB closed, the first YA-9 was brought back to Edwards to become part of the Air Force Flight Test Center Museum. Currently it is in storage, although in actuality it is not in as bad a condition as it appears (all the parts are nearby, just waiting to be reassembled). The location of the engine nacelles shows up well in this photo. (Dennis R. Jenkins)

was accomplished automatically with normal rudder application by the pilot.

If the pilot commanded a move to the left, the SFC system would deflect the rudder to the right, opposite to the usual direction. At the same time, the left speedbrake would open, preventing the aircraft from turning to the right. Instead, the thrust of the rudder would move the aircraft bodily to the left, without turning or banking. With SFC, the pilot could track a ground target without constantly worrying about the bank angle and fuselage direction changes that accompany a conventional turn. Northrop estimated that SFC could double the tracking accuracy of a typical attack. This feature could be selectively engaged or disengaged by the pilot.

The YA-10 was manufactured by the Fairchild-Republic Company. The aircraft used a low-wing, low tail configuration with two high-bypass ratio turbofan engines installed in nacelles mounted on

The titanium "bathtub" that protects the A-10 pilot makes up 47% of the aircraft's armor and can withstand hits from 23mm projectiles fired by the Soviet ZSU-23-4 anti-aircraft gun. The unit consists of massive plates of titanium alloy bolted together and covered with a multi-layered nylon liner which prevents splinters from entering the cockpit even if the bathtub's integrity is compromised. The A-9 featured a similar scheme for protecting the pilot. (Cradle of Aviation Museum via Ken Neubeck)

pylons extending from the upper aft fuselage. Twin vertical stabilizers were mounted on the outboard tips of the horizontal stabilizer. The forward-retracting tricycle landing gear was equipped with an anti-skid system and a steerable nose wheel. The nose gear was offset to the right to permit the firing barrel of the cannon to be on the aircraft

The first YA-10 shows the original shape of the vertical stabilizers. The bottom leading edge would be rounder on production aircraft. Otherwise there were very few external changes. This flight carried a full load of 500-pound bombs on all weapon stations. The exhaust from the auxiliary power unit (APU) is just below the left engine, and tends to leave a black stain on the bottom of the left engine nacelle. By the time this photo was taken this aircraft had been retrofitted with the GAU-8/A 30mm cannon (the nozzles of the interim 20mm cannon did not protrude very far from the nose of the aircraft). This aircraft was painted an overall light grey and carried conventional Air Force markings on the fuselage and wings. The TF34 engines for the first two aircraft were borrowed from the Navy. (U.S. Air Force)

This is one of the DT&E aircraft being manufactured, evidenced by the test boom protruding from the nose. It is differentiated from the two prototypes by the ventral strakes at the leading edge of the wing-fuselage and the leading edge slats on the inboard wing section. (Cradle of Aviation Museum via Ken Neubeck)

centerline. The nose gear fully retracted into the fuselage while the main gear partially retracted into sponsons in the wings. This makes the A-10, perhaps, the last Air Force aircraft without fully retractable and covered landing gear.

Both of the A-X candidates were delivered to Edwards AFB where they would make their first flights in the hands of company test pilots. The YA-10 was the first to fly, making its maiden flight on 10 May 1972 with Howard "Sam" Nelson at the controls. Its Northrop rival followed on 30 May 1972, flown by the unrelated Lew Nelson. The second YA-10 flew on 21 July, and the second YA-9 joined the program on 23 August 1972.

The manufacturers had five months to fix any significant problems since the fly-off rules prohibited any design changes during the Air Force evaluation unless they were safety critical. As it turned out, the only visible change was made to the YA-10. Not surprisingly, stalling

the aircraft sent turbulent airflow into the TF34s, which responded by flaming out. A fixed slot was fitted to the inboard wing between the fuselage and landing gear sponson to smooth out the airflow, largely solving the problem. A somewhat more dubious distinction went to the second YA-10A which was involved in the only incident of the test program, blowing both main tires in a hard landing and sustaining minor damage to its nose wheel. None of this impacted the fly-off competition.

A specially formed Air Force joint test force (JTF) began evaluating the aircraft on 24 October 1972. The JTF, like a similar unit formed a few months earlier to test the F-15, was a new concept for the Air Force. It comprised three test pilots from Air Force Systems Command (AFSC), which was responsible for the engineering and procurement of all Air Force aircraft, and two pilots from TAC, the ultimate user of the A-X. Other experts were assigned from the Air Force Logistics Command and the Air Training

Command to assess the maintenance and training requirements for the competing aircraft. The evaluation was planned to include at least 123 hours flying for each type, and eventually the two YA-9s flew a total of 146 hours in 92 sorties, while the Republic aircraft logged 138.5 hours in 87 sorties. Almost half the flight time was spent firing 20,000 rounds from the interim M61 cannon and dropping 700 "iron" bombs. No precision guided ("smart") weapons were used during the test program.

Although possessing a few handling quirks, the YA-10 was generally preferred by the JTF pilots, but its major advantage was easier access to its underwing hard points. Due mostly to its unique configuration, the A-10 was felt to be more maintainable, and significantly more survivable, than the A-9. The A-10 also exhibited superior maintenance characteristics and better redundancy, but it is unclear how heavily these factors were weighted since it was known from the beginning that the YA-10s were being manu-

Seen from the air traffic control tower at Edwards, one of the DT&E aircraft shows the configuration which would be committed to production. The short pylon under the canopy is the mounting location for the AAS-35(V) PAVE PENNY laser receiver pod. Most test aircraft were equipped with the long flight test boom on the nose. The long straight wing and landing gear sponsons are noteworthy. (Dennis R. Jenkins via the Mick Roth Collection)

factured close to production standards while the YA-9s were truly prototypes.

The YA-9 had its own advantages, the most notable being its unique SFC system. Even though the A-10 was preferred by most of the test pilots, the Northrop aircraft was judged to have generally superior handling characteristics, with significantly less roll inertia. In the final evaluation, both aircraft types exceeded all of the Air Force's requirements.

The decision, however, was far from a foregone conclusion. While the fly-off was unquestionably important, it was not the only factor in the evaluation. The Air Force Systems Command carried out a theoretical assessment of the aircraft in parallel with the fly-off, covering areas which flight testing could not safely explore. An unprecedented series of tests was carried out where representative components of both A-X designs were bombarded with 23mm shells from a Soviet-built anti-aircraft gun to determine how their armor and foam-filled fuel tanks would hold up. Other evaluations included industrial considerations, such as the amount of work needed to set up production, and the ability of each type to be further developed or modified in the future.

There were still other considerations in 1973. Awarding the A-X contract to Republic meant much needed employment for the company and New York, needs that were less urgent for Northrop and Southern California. The aircraft industry in New York had historically been dominated by Republic and Grumman, and the latter was in serious trouble with the F-14 program, putting its future in doubt. Republic had been the largest single subcontractor on the Boeing SST program which had been cancelled in 1971, and the common argument, at least in Congress, was that unless the A-X was awarded to Republic, Long Island's aerospace industry would suffer permanent damage.

It also was not in the Air Force's best interest to allow a major defense contractor to go out of business. Until the 1990s the military was very interested in maintaining its "industrial base" to promote competition and independent research. The military had come to expect at least half-a-dozen responses from qualified suppliers to any of its RFPs. Other things being equal, this factor would tend to favor Fairchild-Republic.

Four of the DT&E aircraft line up with the first YA-10 (last aircraft in line) on the ramp at Edwards AFB. Each of the first eight A-10s carried a different paint scheme in an attempt to find the optimal camouflage for the production aircraft. (Fairchild-Republic)

One of the YA-10A DT&E aircraft used a very unusual paint scheme that looked like half the aircraft could use a good washing. This is the "clean" side of the aircraft, while the far wing and engine nacelle show the appearance of the "dirty" side. (Dennis R. Jenkins via the Mick Roth Collection)

On 18 January 1973 Fairchild-Republic was announced the winner and was awarded a $159,279,888 cost-plus-incentive-fee contract for ten YA-10A development, test, and evaluation (DT&E) aircraft for further testing. Two additional airframes, one for ultimate static load tests and the other for long-term fatigue testing, were also ordered. The preproduction contract included an option for the first 48 production aircraft, but

these would not be ordered until further testing had been completed, and the effectiveness of the GAU-8 had been demonstrated. The estimated unit cost of production A-10As was $1.5 million in FY70 dollars, based on a buy of 600 aircraft to be delivered at the rate of 20 per month.

The two losing Northrop YA-9 pro-

totypes were turned over to NASA but were never used by the agency. Both aircraft were later transferred to museums. The first prototype went to the Castle AFB museum until the base was closed, then it was returned to Edwards AFB as part of the Air Force Flight Test Museum collection. The second prototype is in the March Field, California, museum.

General Electric received a $27,666,900 firm-fixed-price contract for 32 TF34 engines for the ten DT&E aircraft. The engine contract was not a foregone conclusion either, since an Avco-powered A-10 and a GE-powered A-9 had both been studied. Avco Lycoming was also offering a developed version of the F102 with greater power and growth potential, and the F102 was significantly less expensive. However, no military aircraft used the F102, and the Air Force wanted to minimize the number of different engine types in service. The TF34, on the other hand, was going to be used on a proposed eight TF34-engined AWACS and potentially byother aircraft. The TF34 had also been derived from the TF39 used on the Lockheed C-5 Galaxy, and

The two YA-10s (#1 shown here) were initially equipped with the tried-and-true General Electric M61A1 Vulcan 20mm cannon. This cannon had a significantly smaller muzzle that did not protrude as far from the nose as the final 30mm cannon. Compare the lack of vents in the side of the fuselage to later aircraft. The test aircraft usually flew with test booms with alpha and beta probes. (Dennis R. Jenkins via the Mick Roth Collection)

WARBIRD**TECH**
S E R I E S

shared some commonality with that unit. As it ended up, the engine was only used in the S-3, A-10 and, in civil form, the Canadair Challenger 601. But it also formed the basis for the later F404 and F110 engines.

Republic and GE worked together on a package of low risk modifications to the TF34 which would reduce its cost without degrading its performance. Modifications to the engine for the A-10 were very minor, mainly to allow the engine to be interchangeable between the left and right pylons. Unique upward angled exhaust pipes were developed to reduce trim changes when power was

adjusted. The two prototype A-10s flew with Navy-standard engines, but preproduction aircraft received the slightly heavier and less expensive TF34-GE-100s. However, heavier-than-anticipated use, dictated by more hard-turning low-level flight than had been envisioned, resulted in greater-than-expected hot section wear and tear. As a result, engines were upgraded to TF34-GE-100A standards with a modified combustor

and high pressure turbine, doubling hot section life to 2,000 hours, including 360 hours at maximum power. The new engine uses a novel nickel alloy combustor which gives a long, maintenance-free life, while the fuel injection system uses a two-stage swirler which vaporizes the fuel before ignition.

The second YA-10 was used for the spin test series. A spin recovery parachute was fitted on the aft fuselage in case the aircraft could not be recovered from a spin using the flight controls. To aid in photography, one wing and tail were painted white.
(Mick Roth)

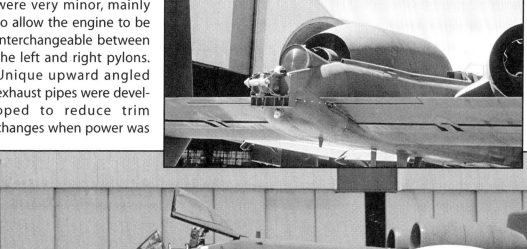

BATTLE DAMAGE

The Vought (LTV) A-7D was built in a plant in Grand Prairie, Texas, just outside Dallas. With production winding down, the plant was looking for additional A-7 sales. The Texas congressional delegation began to push the A-7D as a close air support aircraft, arguing the A-10 was not necessary when an existing aircraft could meet the requirements. In July 1973, when the Air Force was slow to act on the congressional recommendation that the A-10 be evaluated against the A-7D, funding for four of the preproduction YA-10As was cut by Congress. The Air Force finally agreed to conduct the fly-off from 15 April until 10 May 1974 at McConnell AFB and Fort Riley, Kansas. The second YA-10 and an A-7D were flown by four Air Force pilots with combat experience in F-100s and F-4s. Since this was a prototype A-10, it was still not fitted with the 30mm cannon, heads-up display (HUD), Maverick missile launch systems, or any countermeasures equipment. Nevertheless, because of its design, the YA-10 was found to be more survivable, less expensive to operate, and more deadly. Perhaps the most impressive result was that the YA-10, carrying eighteen 500-pound bombs, was able to spend two hours "on station" 300 miles from base. The A-7D was only able to spend 11 minutes. Army and Air Force testimony to Congress after the trials was unanimous in stating that the A-10 was the only viable aircraft for the CAS mission. The final report was delivered to Congress in June 1974. This finally killed the proposed A-7DER, a stretched Corsair II incorporating the GAU-8 30mm cannon.

While awaiting the first preproduction aircraft, testing proceeded using the two prototypes. The two YA-10s continued to fly at Edwards throughout the rest of 1973 and 1974, although at a slightly lower rate than in 1972. The second YA-10 conducted a spin test series during late 1974 and also tested a package of aerodynamic changes which reduced drag in both cruising and maneuvering flight. The wingspan was increased by 30 inches, the canopy and windscreen shapes were altered slightly, the engine pylons were shortened and streamlined, and the landing gear sponsons were reduced in cross-section. The Air Force had intended to replace the fixed slats that had been temporarily installed during the test program with automatic fully retractable units, but this proved to be too costly, and was not done.

During the first part of 1974, the Air Force began expressing concerns with the lack of progress in gearing up production. Most of the blame was placed on the obsolete tooling and procedures used by the Republic factory, which was hardly surprising since Farmingdale had not run a major program since the

The flight test boom was fitted into the area normally occupied by the air refueling receptacle. The DT&E aircraft also added provisions to carry the PAVE PENNY pod on a short pylon on the right side of the fuselage. This pod is not a laser designator, and simply detects reflected laser energy to provide additional cues on the A-10's heads-up display to aid the pilot in hitting the target. The A-10 might be the last American combat aircraft equipped with a "framed" windscreen. (Dennis R. Jenkins)

Due to the location of the engines above and behind the wing, they were subject to losing airflow when the wing was stalled at high angles-of-attack. Fitting slats to the inboard leading edge of the wing cured the problem, and both prototypes and all DT&E aircraft were retrofitted with fixed slats. Partially retractable units that automatically deploy based on air pressure were tried later and found to offer less base drag. Fully retractable units were going to be used on production aircraft but were cancelled for cost reasons. (Mick Roth)

closure of the F-105 production line more than 10 years earlier. Both the cost and schedule targets of the program were in jeopardy. An Air Force inquiry led to a series of changes in Republic production management, and the Air Force increased its oversight staff at Farmingdale. Republic responded by acquiring new numerically controlled machine tools, and subcontracting some critical machined components with outside vendors. The cost of this modernization was a blow to Republic, which badly needed the funds to improve its business base.

By mid-1974 good progress was being made with A-10 testing and evaluation, and the development of the GAU-8/A was also going well, although it had yet to be fired from the A-10. The Air Force released $39 million to procure long-lead items for 52 production A-10As; the 48 aircraft which had been optioned at the start of the program, plus the four aircraft which Congress had cut from the original DT&E contract. Five months later, with more aircraft and weapon trials completed and the DT&E aircraft in final assembly, production of the A-10 was unconditionally authorized by the DoD.

The first YA-10 prototype was retrofitted with the GAU-8/A in September 1974. Test firings were conducted against 15 U.S. M48s and Soviet T-62s. Strikes against the side and top of the T-62s, not only with the API ammunition but also with the HEI shells, penetrated the tanks' armor and set off secondary explosions of internal fuel and ammunition. This was a pleasant but unexpected surprise since the HEI ammunition had originally been designed for use against softer-skinned vehicles. Impressively, the GAU-8's velocity is such that ballistic drop and windage can be largely ignored, even at long ranges.

The leading edge slat in their fully extended position. Compare this to the slats in their fully retracted position in the photo at the top of the page. This type of automatic slat has been found on combat aircraft since World War II and has proven to be very effective, inexpensive, and generally reliable, although the A-10's retraction mechanism tends to stick. (Mick Roth)

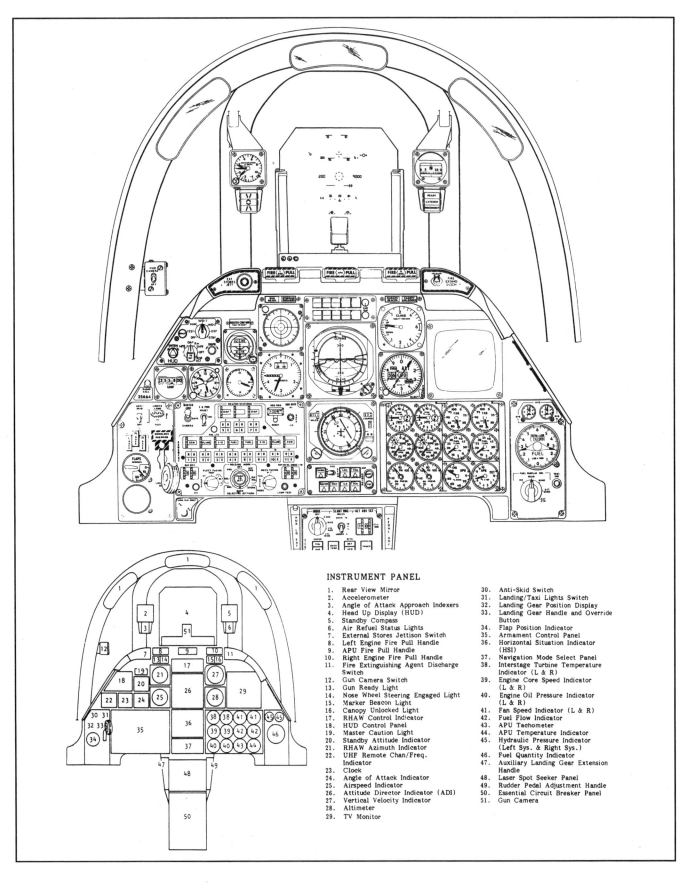

INSTRUMENT PANEL

1. Rear View Mirror
2. Accelerometer
3. Angle of Attack Approach Indexers
4. Head Up Display (HUD)
5. Standby Compass
6. Air Refuel Status Lights
7. External Stores Jettison Switch
8. Left Engine Fire Pull Handle
9. APU Fire Pull Handle
10. Right Engine Fire Pull Handle
11. Fire Extinguishing Agent Discharge Switch
12. Gun Camera Switch
13. Gun Ready Light
14. Nose Wheel Steering Engaged Light
15. Marker Beacon Light
16. Canopy Unlocked Light
17. RHAW Control Indicator
18. HUD Control Panel
19. Master Caution Light
20. Standby Attitude Indicator
21. RHAW Azimuth Indicator
22. UHF Remote Chan/Freq. Indicator
23. Clock
24. Angle of Attack Indicator
25. Airspeed Indicator
26. Attitude Director Indicator (ADI)
27. Vertical Velocity Indicator
28. Altimeter
29. TV Monitor

30. Anti-Skid Switch
31. Landing/Taxi Lights Switch
32. Landing Gear Position Display
33. Landing Gear Handle and Override Button
34. Flap Position Indicator
35. Armament Control Panel
36. Horizontal Situation Indicator (HSI)
37. Navigation Mode Select Panel
38. Interstage Turbine Temperature Indicator (L & R)
39. Engine Core Speed Indicator (L & R)
40. Engine Oil Pressure Indicator (L & R)
41. Fan Speed Indicator (L & R)
42. Fuel Flow Indicator
43. APU Tachometer
44. APU Temperature Indicator
45. Hydraulic Pressure Indicator (Left Sys. & Right Sys.)
46. Fuel Quantity Indicator
47. Auxiliary Landing Gear Extension Handle
48. Laser Spot Seeker Panel
49. Rudder Pedal Adjustment Handle
50. Essential Circuit Breaker Panel
51. Gun Camera

The A-10 has a truly simple cockpit arrangement. Only the radar warning display and the Maverick TV screen would not be instantly recognizable to an F-84 pilot. (U.S. Air Force)

The cannon's 10,000-pound recoil would prove unacceptable unless the firing barrel was mounted on the aircraft's centerline. Because only one barrel fires at a time, the cannon still appears to be offset slightly to the left. Even with the asymmetric recoil force cancelled out, firing the cannon has a very noticeable effect, reducing the aircraft's speed by several knots. The 30mm GAU-8/A's 17,700 muzzle horsepower compares to less than 100 muzzle horsepower for a typical World War II 20mm cannon. Muzzle horsepower is a factor of muzzle velocity, projectile mass, and rate of fire, and gives an excellent idea of the power being generated. An automatic elevator pitch down feature had been developed to prevent unwanted attitude changes during cannon firing. This feature was found unnecessary during the tests, and was eliminated from production aircraft. The GAU-8/A was certified for use on the A-10A in July 1974.

A potentially serious problem was uncovered once flight testing with the cannon began. The explosive gases generated by the propellant were not being fully burned in the barrel, and the remnants were being expelled and ignited in front of the aircraft, forming a large fireball. An early solution was to weld massive square-section vents on the nose, but while this allowed firing trials to continue, it clearly would not be an acceptable fix for production aircraft.

The original propellant used by the 30mm ammunition caused secondary gun gas ignition (SGGI), or instantaneous gas combustion, in

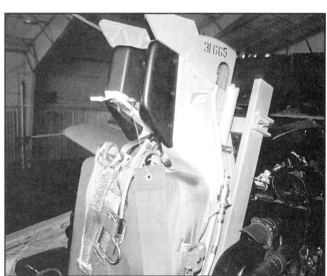

An interesting feature of the A-10 is a location on the left console to store "piddle pack"—small plastic containers that are available for the pilot to relieve himself. A front panel photo is included in the color section. (Mick Roth)

The Battelle device was wicked looking. Its purpose was to create a turbulent airflow around the gun barrels, preventing the gun gases from accumulating while the cannon was fired. About half the operational A-10s in the fleet were fitted with the device before severe cracking was found in the aircraft's primary structure. (Cradle of Aviation Museum via Ken Neubeck)

front of the aircraft. This was the most serious technical problem facing the A-10 program towards the end of 1974, but was solved by adding potassium nitrate to the propellant, a technique borrowed from the Navy's battleship guns. This change very slightly increased the velocity of the projectile, but also left a residue which was injected into the TF34 engines, causing engine stalls, flameouts, and the gradual loss of engine power. While it was testing a new gun propellant on 8 June 1978, both of the last preproduction aircraft's engines flamed out and failed to restart. Its pilot had his ejection filmed by a chase plane and broadcast on the nightly news.

This accident began a long investigation of methods to eliminate the gun gas ingestion problems. With millions of rounds of high residue producing 30mm rounds in war reserve material storage which the A-10 would use during combat, the Air Force recognized the need to find a final solution to the problem. The study was conducted by a joint Republic, General Electric, and Air Force team during late 1980 and early 1981. A number of solutions were proposed: 1) a device to be mounted on the gun muzzle to divert the gun gas; 2) an extended

nose section with a door for deflecting the gas; 3) louvers on the side of the fuselage; 4) frequent engine washes; and 5) continuous engine ignition applied during cannon fire.

The first choice was a device designed to divert gun gas away from the engine. Fairchild-Republic, General Electric, and Battelle Laboratories each designed and produced diverter prototypes. Battelle's design was selected as the most cost efficient since it required the fewest structural modifications,

At the same time the Battelle device was added, most aircraft received fairings over the gun cooling vents in the left side of the fuselage. There are a couple of variations of these vents which can be seen in the various photographs in this book. (Cradle of Aviation Museum via Ken Neubeck)

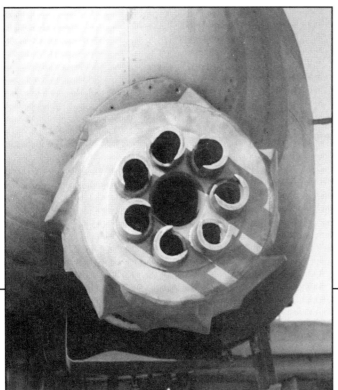

The head-on view of the Battelle device shows the different angle each barrel was cut at. (Cradle of Aviation Museum via Ken Neubeck)

Although fairly successful at dispersing the gun gases that were causing flameouts, the Battelle device had its own set of problems. The most significant was that the torque it put on the cannon caused various areas of the A-10's structure to develop cracks that could not economically be fixed. The device was removed shortly after the cracks were discovered, and all that remains of the modification is the two-piece gun housing panel around the barrels. (U.S. Air Force)

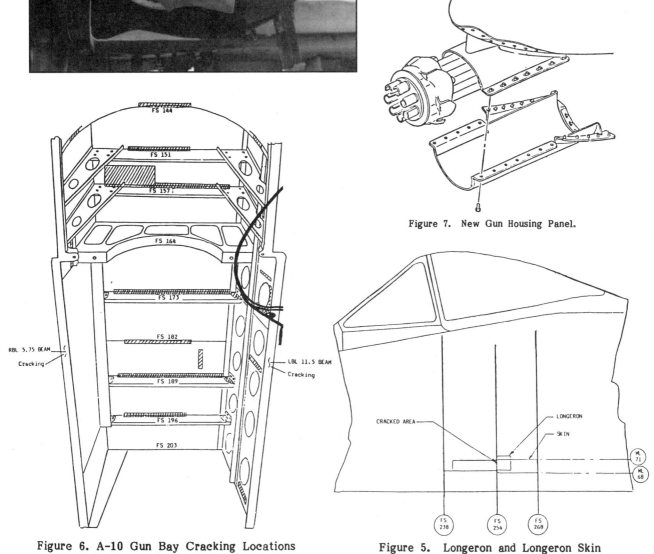

Figure 7. New Gun Housing Panel.

Figure 6. A-10 Gun Bay Cracking Locations
View Looking Up and Aft.

Figure 5. Longeron and Longeron Skin
Cracking Locations.

Yet another attempt to cure the gun gas ingestion problem was a redesigned forward fuselage that completely covered the gun barrels. A vent opened above the barrels to duct in air that was mixed with the gun gas and vented overboard under the fuselage. This reportedly was a very effective solution, but it was not cost effective to modify the entire A-10 fleet to the new shape. (Cradle of Aviation Museum via Ken Neubeck)

or at least that was the theory. Battelle manufactured 20 prototype GFU-16/A gun gas diverters, then turned the design over to Wayne Colony and Contour of California for the production contract. Eventually 750 diverters were built between 1984 and 1988, although not all of them were installed. The Battelle diverter was a medieval-looking device that attached to the front of the GAU-8/A barrels, outside the aircraft. It produced a turbulent airflow around the nose of the aircraft, dispersing the gas cloud and sending it further away from the fuselage, and usually outside the ingestion envelope for the engines.

Unfortunately, there were some serious unwelcome side-effects. Structural cracking was discovered on modified aircraft, resulting in further checking. It was eventually found that all modified aircraft were exhibiting similar cracking around the UHF/ADF antenna, the aft gun mount, the lower left longeron skin, the lower left longeron just below the boarding ladder, and the gun bay. Since the A-10 was out of production and Republic itself had ceased to exist, there was a very limited supply of spare longerons. Modifications were suspended, and the Air Force ordered the gun gas diverters removed from all aircraft.

The solutions to some of the cracking problems were relatively simple. For instance, the UHF/ADF antenna received new isolated shock-mounts, curing the problem. All A-10s received the new antenna mounts between 1987 and 1989. An improved aft gun mount was installed that used a sacrificial bushing to absorb the severe firing loads. This bushing requires replacement after approximately 10,000 rounds, but prevents the aft mount and surrounding structure from cracking.

At first the solution to the longeron skin and longeron cracking also appeared relatively simple. The

The circular hole and panel with two rows of five vents is part of the gun cooling system added during the ill-fated Battelle device period. The sharkmouth is the symbol of the 23rd TASS "Flying Tigers" which was one of the main operators of the A-10 during the Gulf War. (Mick Roth)

original 0.050-inch thick aluminum skin was replaced with 0.100-inch thick stainless steel skin. This was intended to reduce the stresses exerted on the longeron itself, but the skin proved too brittle and most aircraft never received the modification. The Air Force ordered additional spare longerons from a new supplier to repair any aircraft deemed unflightworthy. Eventually, the Air Force abandoned all attempts to use the Battelle device.

Two remnants of the Battelle modification did survive on all operational aircraft, however. The first is a two-piece gun housing panel that covers the barrels immediately in front of the nose. The other is a barrel cooling unit that attempts to evenly cool the barrels to minimize bullet dispersion. During GAU-8/A firing, three of the seven barrels always have their firing breeches

closed because a spent or unspent case is chambered. Free stream airflow can not provide cooling through these barrels. The barrel cooling unit rotates the barrels immediately after the cannon has stopped firing to allow cooling air to flow around the hot barrels. If the pilot engages the trigger during the cooling cycle, the rotation is immediately halted and cannon fires normally after a very brief (a fraction of a second) hesitation. The time required to come up to full firing rate is the same (0.55 second) as an unmodified cannon. Aircraft equipped with this modification

have an access panel with numerous holes on the lower left side of the fuselage. Over the years there have been a variety of different fairings installed around and over this panel to smooth out the airflow.

Since the diverter was apparently never going to live up to its promise, the second choice modification was a forward fuselage that extended completely over the cannon barrels, and included a special vent door that opened when the cannon was being fired. This changed the profile of the extreme forward fuselage, and did mitigate most of the problem. However it was deemed uneconomical and was not pursued further.

The last alternatives were the least attractive, at least operationally. The

The current (1998) configuration of fairings looks like this. The "Desert Storm" nose art is noteworthy. The art ("Fist") on the other side of the fuselage is shown at the top of page 90. This aircraft is currently in the McClellan AFB museum. (Mick Roth)

Its easy to see why gun gas ingestion could be a problem on the A-10. The rate of fire, combined with the large quantity of propellant needed to get the 30mm projectiles moving at high velocity, produces a lot of gas in front of the aircraft. Before the potassium nitrate was added to the propellant, this gas contained a high percentage of unburned powder which caused a large fireball to erupt in front of the pilot! (U.S. Air Force)

engines were equipped with a system that engaged continuous ignition during trigger activation and for 30 seconds after the trigger was released. Although this causes a higher-than-expected failure rate amongst the engine igniters, it was a relatively small (and inexpensive) price to pay to minimize the flame-outs. The gradual loss of engine power was solved by using clean water to wash the engines after every thousand rounds fired. A more elegant solution was never found, and gun gas ingestion has remained a concern throughout the A-10's career.

The first DT&E aircraft was completed at Farmingdale in late 1974, and after preliminary ground tests it was partially disassembled and flown to Edwards AFB in a C-5A transport. It made its first flight on 15 February 1975, a day after the 1,000th YA-10 flight hour had been recorded. The first DT&E aircraft was not fitted with a cannon, instead carrying temperature, vibration, and strain sensors linked to a central digital recording system. The aircraft would be used to evaluate aerodynamic performance, and handling.

Although externally similar to the YA-10s, a number of subtle changes were incorporated into the preproduction aircraft, mostly around the wings. Fixed leading edge slats and trailing-edge fairings, which were found to be necessary to avoid stalling the engines when the wing stalled, were standardized. Ventral strakes that had been added to the prototypes to smooth airflow around the fuselage weapon pylons were also standardized. The wingspan was increased 30 inches outboard of the ailerons, and maximum flap deflection was cut from 40° to 30° (and eventually just 20° on production aircraft). Finally, the vertical stabilizers were reshaped, an air refueling receptacle was added in the nose, as was an internal boarding ladder, and the cannon was depressed 2 degrees. A small pylon was also added on the side of the fuselage for a AAS-35(V)

Large ventral strakes were added to smooth the airflow coming off the fuselage sides before it impinged on the fuselage weapons stations. These strakes were hastily added to the two YA-10s, and became production features on the YA-10A DT&E aircraft. The fuselage stations can only carry gravity weapons, not missiles of any kind. (Mick Roth)

PAVE PENNY laser receiver. The six preproduction aircraft were designated YA-10A, versus the YA-10 designation (no 'A' suffix) carried by the original two prototypes.

Each of the six preproduction aircraft was tasked with a specific part of the test program. The second preproduction aircraft was the first A-10 to make its maiden flight from Republic's Farmingdale facility, on 26 April 1975, and was the first aircraft equipped with a complete avionics suite in order to perform armament and weapons certification. The third preproduction aircraft was dedicated to subsystem tests and weapons delivery, and made its maiden flight on 10 June 1975. The fourth and fifth aircraft performed the initial operational test and evalu-

The first prototype was transferred to the Rome Laboratory in early 1977. It has been used to evaluate various antenna configurations, ECM pods, and even LANTIRN pods. (Air Force Research Laboratory)

ation (IOT&E) series and first flew on 17 July 1975 and 9 August 1975, respectively. The final preproduction aircraft made its maiden flight on 10 September 1975, and was the climate test aircraft. All the DT&E

aircraft except the first and fourth were equipped with the GAU-8/A cannon. Each of the six DT&E aircraft also wore a different camouflage scheme to test various ideas although none were adopted for the operational aircraft. The prototype and pre-production aircraft used the ESCAPAC ejection seat, while production aircraft switched to the ACES II.

The most severe event to mar the A-10's early success was the fatal crash of an aircraft at the 1977 Paris Air Salon at Le Bourget. Test Pilot Sam Nelson was killed when he hit the ground during a series of low-level loops on 3 June 1977, a grave loss to the program. (Cradle of Aviation Museum via Ken Neubeck)

When the second preproduction A-10 made its first flight from Farmingdale, it was the first new aircraft to fly from Farmingdale since the last F-105 was completed. Fairchild, however, had sold the Republic airfield for general-aviation use some years before, and it was considered too crowded to be used for acceptance testing. By April, it had been decided to move A-10 final assembly and flight testing to another Fairchild facility at Hagerstown, Maryland. The first 13 aircraft (6 DT&E and 7 production) alternated with the final assembly between Farmingdale and Hagerstown. After that the fuselage and the wing assemblies for each aircraft (the last 699) would be trucked from Farm-

ingdale to Hagerstown for final assembly and flight testing. The completion of the second DT&E aircraft also allowed the first prototype to be retired and placed in "flyable storage" on 15 April 1975 after 467 flights and 590.9 hours. It was dropped from the inventory as salvage on 31 October 1975. The second prototype was withdrawn from the test program in June after being flown a total of 548.5 hours in 354 flights. It later became an Air Force recruiting display before being turned over to the Air Force Museum at Wright-Patterson AFB in Dayton, Ohio.

In late 1976 the first prototype was transferred to Air Force's Rome Air

Development Center at Griffiths AFB, New York. It was partially disassembled, transported by rail from Edwards AFB to Davis-Monthan AFB, and by truck from there to Griffiths AFB. On 27 October 1977 it was mounted on a tower to conduct testing into various aspects of electromagnetic interference. The cannon placement was modified to conform to production aircraft since the original placement had the firing barrel of the GAU-8/A off the centerline. While at the Rome laboratory the YA-10 has been used to evaluate various communications and electronic warfare antenna configurations. At some point, an example of almost every Air Force aircraft finds its way to Rome

for similar testing, including the F-15 and an F-117.

Flight testing gradually began to fall behind schedule since there were only six YA-10As, instead of the expected ten. The first production A-10A made its maiden flight on 10 October 1975 and was delivered to the Air Force on 5 November 1975. The first four production aircraft joined the testing effort, effectively bringing the number of aircraft up to what had been expected, just a little late. The A-10 was a simple aircraft, and testing progressed with relatively few problems. Unfortunately it was determined that the original 2,000 pound weight savings for the DT&E aircraft compared with the original prototypes had been optimistic, and that the A-10A was somewhat overweight. The Air Force, however, decided that the resulting degradation of overall performance was not critical and did not pursue a proposed weight reduction program. The fatigue test airframe suffered a failure during static testing at Farmingdale, but a minor redesign of a forged fuselage/wing fitting solved the problem.

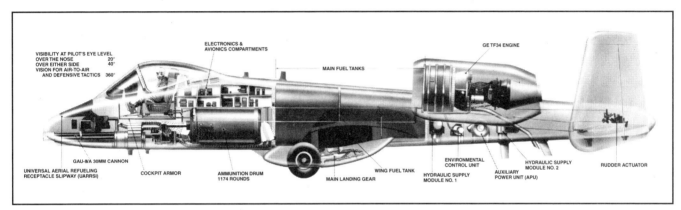

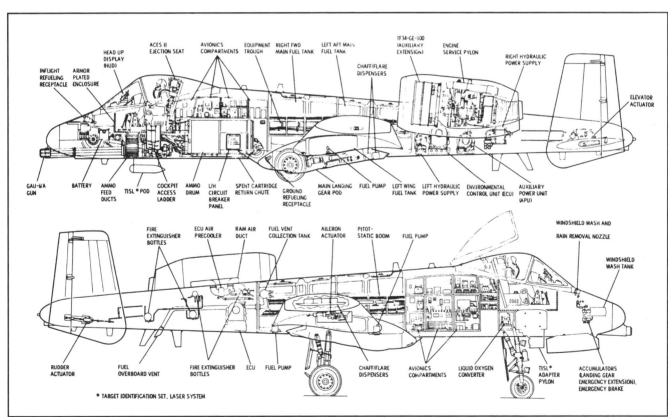

A cutaway reveals the A-10's simple configuration. Long equipment troughs run along each side of the fuselage and are accessed by removing a long line of access panels in the outer skin. The forward fuselage is tightly packed with the pilot, cannon, and avionics, and is also the most heavily armored location on the aircraft. (U.S. Air Force)

'HOGS AT HAGERSTOWN

THE A-10 ENTERS PRODUCTION

All of this delayed the delivery of the first operational A-10A to the 355th TFW until March 1976, five months behind the original schedule. The 355th TFW, based at Davis-Monthan AFB, had been designated the first unit to receive A-10As in November 1974, and conducted the A-10's final operational test and evaluation. The wing also flew several aircraft to Europe for the Farnborough air show, and then on for a tour of Europe. While in Europe, the aircraft took part in various exercises with NATO units to show the capabilities of the new aircraft. Arctic tests (Operation Jack Frost) were conducted at Eielson AFB, Alaska, during January 1977, and in April four aircraft took part in Red Flag exercises at Nellis AFB, operating from a dry lakebed. Later in 1977 the Joint Attack Weapons System (JAWS) operation defined the A-10A's tactic, particularly how the

A-10 would operate in conjunction with Army attack helicopters. Several of the JAWS A-10s received very interesting paint schemes in yet another attempt to find the optimal camouflage. In April 1979 the 355th was redesignated a Tactical Training Wing (TTW), and would subsequently train all A-10 crews.

The build-up of production at the Hagerstown facility was slow, and it was 3 April 1978 before the 100th production A-10A was completed. Production continued with aircraft buys in each year from FY75 through FY82. A total of 2 YA-10s, 6 YA-10As, and 708 A-10As were manufactured. The only thing to mar the A-10's early success was the fatal crash of an aircraft at the 1977 Paris Air Salon at Le Bourget. Sam Nelson was killed when he hit the ground during a series of low-level loops on 3 June 1977, a grave loss to the program.

The production A-10A retained the same unusual external configuration as the prototypes. The high aspect ratio unswept wing has a large thickness/chord ratio and is highly cambered to produce lift. The wing structure is extremely strong but relatively light weight. The outer wing panels incorporate approximately 7° of dihedral, and a low wing loading gives excellent turning performance. The wings have anhedral Hoerner wingtips that reduce induced drag and wingtip vortices, and also improve aileron effectiveness at low speeds.

The cockpit is set high on the extreme forward fuselage, resulting in excellent visibility forward and down, a desirable characteristic for a successful ground attack aircraft. The cockpit itself is remarkably austere, a radar warning receiver and the TV monitor for the Maverick missile being the only major fea-

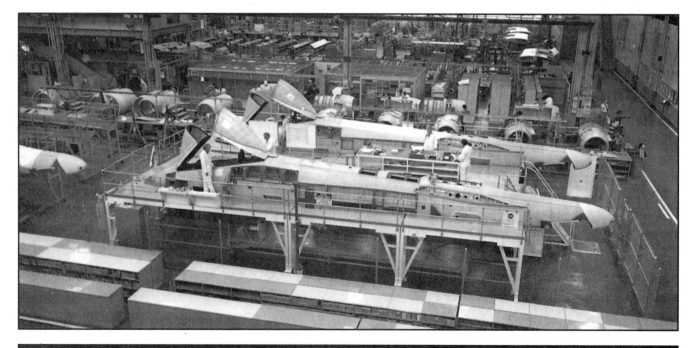

tures that would not be immediately familiar to an F-84 pilot.

Two-thirds of all battle damage was designed to be repairable in the field within 12 hours, and three-quarters within 24 hours. During the Vietnam War, Republic had been forced to make hasty modifications to its F-105s to allow them to remain controllable after sustaining damage to the flight control system (this reflected design philosophies prevalent for the F-105's original nuclear strike mission). Operations in direct support of ground forces would undoubtedly expose the A-10 to significant

The A-10 assembly line was not particularly hi-tech—in fact, the Air Force had serious concerns over the state of the line when production first began. Fairchild-Republic did, at the Air Force's insistence, invest in numeric-controlled milling machines and other state-of-the-art equipment, but the line still did not reflect its counterparts at Boeing or McDonnell Douglas. Of course, the A-10 was a much simpler aircraft than anything being manufactured at the other aerospace giants. The A-10 would be the last aircraft mass-manufactured by the old Republic organization. Noteworthy is that the front windscreen hinges forward to allow access to the instrument panel. (Cradle of Aviation Museum via Ken Neubeck)

During the Joint Attack Weapons System (JAWS) operation at Nellis in 1977, several A-10s were painted in unusual "spot" camouflage using various shades of greens and browns. A sample of the paint schemes is shown here.
(top of this page by Mike Henning; all others by Mick Roth)

WARBIRD**TECH**
S E R I E S

The entire bottom of the forward fuselage opens to allow access to the GAU-8/A 30mm cannon and its ammunition drum. The black protrusion on the left is an antenna for the ALR-46 radar warning set. (Cradle of Aviation Museum via Ken Neubeck)

amounts of ground fire, hence an emphasis on survivability. Single point failures were minimized, accounting for two engines and vertical stabilizers, and for the profusion of duplicated systems, hydraulics, and fuel lines. These redundant systems are generally widely separated and carried in protected ducts. If all hydraulic systems are lost, the flight controls revert to a manual system where the pilot's controls are mechanically linked to the rudder, elevator, and aileron trim tabs. This provides a control system with limited authority, but one which can bring a damaged aircraft back successfully. If one side of a flight control surface jams, it can be disconnected in flight and the other side operated normally. Interestingly the Air Force battle damage repair manual indicates that a broomstick can be used to replace a damaged control rod, and such a repair was actually made to a yaw control rod during Operation Desert Storm.

The wings and horizontal stabilizers each have triple spars, giving an significant degree of structural redundancy. The main landing gear is housed in sponsons to avoid the need for a wheel well inside the wing, which would necessitate breaks in the wing structure. The engines are set high to avoid debris ingestion during operation from semi-prepared strips, and are widely separated to avoid damage to one affecting the other. Very few

The large equipment troughs along the fuselage sides show up well in this assembly line photo. (Cradle of Aviation Museum via Ken Neubeck)

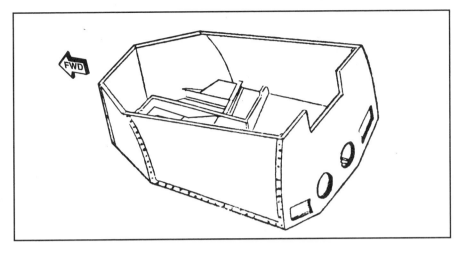

The infamous titanium "bathtub" that protects the pilot of the A-10. The openings in the back of the armor are for electrical, hydraulic, and control system access to the cockpit. (U.S. Air Force)

external skin panels use double curvature, and the majority of the A-10A's skin consists of simple flat plates, cylinders, or cones which require no expensive and time consuming stretch-forming during manufacture, and are easier to repair in the field. Most major components including the engine, vertical stabilizers, and landing gear were interchangeable between the left and right sides of the aircraft. Unlike most fighter aircraft, the A-10 has no tailhook or drag chute.

Agility also makes a major contribution to survivability since it

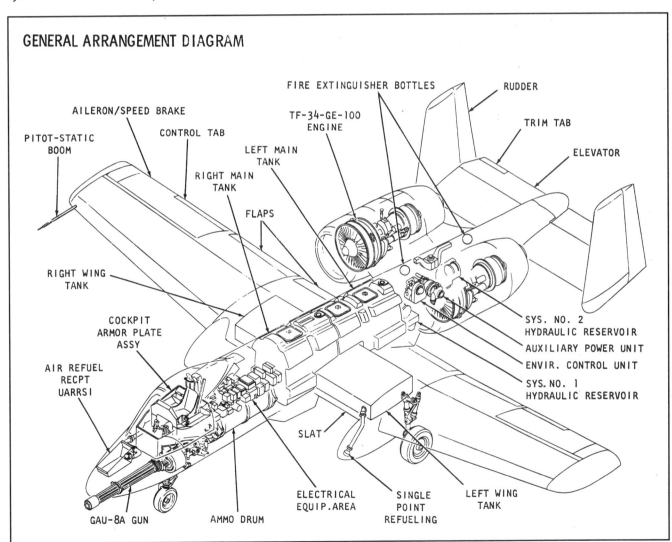

GENERAL ARRANGEMENT DIAGRAM

All of the A-10's fuel is concentrated around the wing-fuselage junction where changes in quantity have a minimal affect on the aircraft's center-of-gravity. (U.S. Air Force)

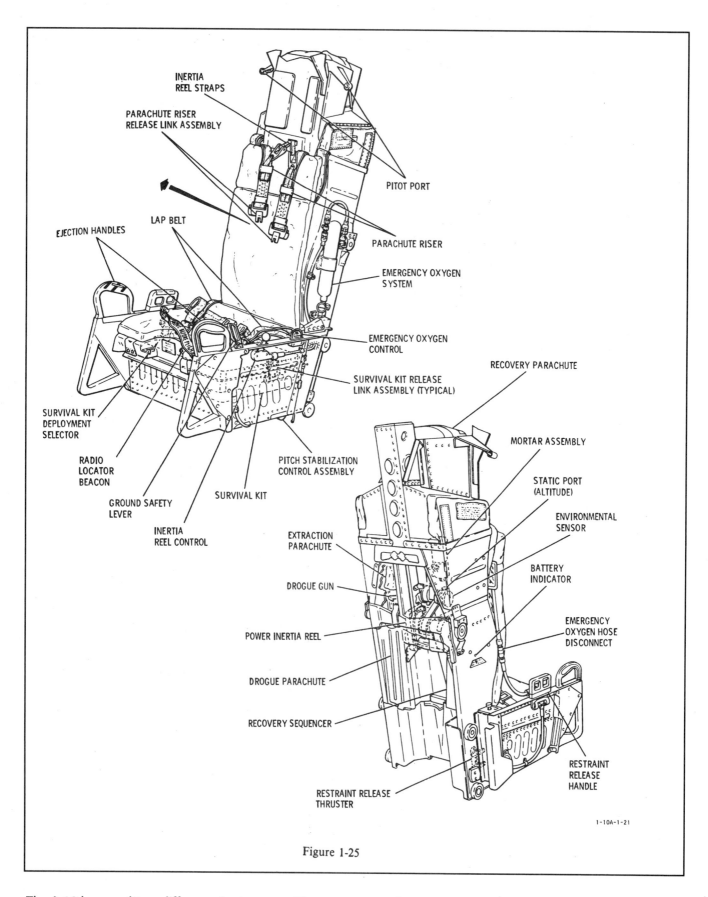

INERTIA
REEL STRAPS

PARACHUTE RISER
RELEASE LINK ASSEMBLY

PITOT PORT

EJECTION HANDLES

LAP BELT

PARACHUTE RISER

EMERGENCY OXYGEN
SYSTEM

EMERGENCY OXYGEN
CONTROL

SURVIVAL KIT RELEASE
LINK ASSEMBLY (TYPICAL)

RECOVERY PARACHUTE

SURVIVAL KIT
DEPLOYMENT
SELECTOR

RADIO
LOCATOR
BEACON

PITCH STABILIZATION
CONTROL ASSEMBLY

MORTAR ASSEMBLY

STATIC PORT
(ALTITUDE)

GROUND SAFETY
LEVER

SURVIVAL KIT

ENVIRONMENTAL
SENSOR

INERTIA
REEL CONTROL

EXTRACTION
PARACHUTE

BATTERY
INDICATOR

DROGUE GUN

POWER INERTIA REEL

EMERGENCY
OXYGEN HOSE
DISCONNECT

DROGUE PARACHUTE

RECOVERY SEQUENCER

RESTRAINT RELEASE
THRUSTER

RESTRAINT
RELEASE
HANDLE

1-10A-1-21

Figure 1-25

The A-10 has used two different ejection seats. The prototype and preproduction aircraft used the ESCAPAC ejection seat, while production aircraft switched to the ACES II, shown here in the flight manual illustration. (U.S. Air Force)

The first few operational aircraft to arrive at Davis-Monthan AFB near Tucson used large black tail codes and carried their national insignia on the engine nacelle. (Mick Roth)

Later, much smaller tail codes would be used and the national insignia moved to the forward fuselage. An ALQ-119 ECM pod is on the right wing. (Don Logan via the Mick Roth Collection)

allows the A-10 to make maximum use of terrain masking to avoid exposing itself to hostile fire. Relatively low speed turns produce a small turn radius and high turn rate. For example, an A-10 making a 3.5g 180° turn at 320 knots will complete the turn in 16 seconds with a radius of 2,700 feet, while an F-16 traveling at 600 knots and pulling 6g will take 17 seconds with a radius of 3,620 feet.

The A-10A's cockpit is surrounded with a titanium "bathtub" designed to withstand hits from 23mm projectiles from the Soviet ZSU-23-4, and even to withstand some 57mm strikes. The bathtub is not a casting, as the name might suggest, but consists of massive plates of titani-

um alloy bolted together and a multi-layered nylon liner which prevents splinters from entering the cockpit, even if the bathtub's integrity is compromised. Titanium was chosen after an extensive evaluation of ceramic and aluminum armor. This single unit represents 47% of the weight of armor carried, with 37% more protecting the fuel system. Most of the remainder covers the 30mm ammunition drum.

The A-10's internal fuel capacity is 1,650 U.S. gallons, which weighs approximately 10,700 pounds. The main fuel tanks form a cross in the center-section of the wing/fuselage, close to the center of gravity. The tanks are tear-resistant and self-sealing, and are divided into

separate, independent units that are isolated from one another. A pair of self-sealing sump tanks contains sufficient fuel for a 230 mile flight in the event that all the main fuel tanks are damaged. The tanks are protected by rigid, reinforced fire-retardant foam, with a layer of reticulated flexible foam inside to minimize spillage of fuel, prevent airflow through a holed tank, and to inhibit fire. During testing, over 300 rounds of high-explosive incendiary (HEI) ammunition were fired into a set of test tanks and failed to cause an explosion.

The aircraft is fitted with a single point refueling receptacle in the front of the left landing gear sponson. Standard over-wing fuel caps allow gravity fueling if necessary at a remote location. The combination of fuel-efficient engines and relatively generous fuel supply allows the A-10 to fly 150 miles, spend one hour on station, then return 150 miles while still maintaining safety reserves. The three inboard pylons are plumbed for fuel tanks, with a single tank carried on the centerline being the most common ferry configuration. The 600-gallon external fuel tanks are the same as those used by the F-111.

No provisions were made in the original design for an inertial navigation system (INS) or weapon delivery computer, reflecting the generally poor reliability associated with the "advanced avionics" used during the aircraft's design period. It did not take long to discover that relying on line-of-sight TACAN was impractical at very low level. By the late 1970s technology had improved remarkably, and the Air Force finally began installation of an AN/ASN-141 inertial navigation system with the 391st aircraft. This also required the installation of a modified HUD with a new, more powerful symbology generator. Interestingly, the A-10A was not originally produced with an autopilot, something that would cause grief to the pilots that had to ferry the aircraft across the Atlantic during Operation Desert Shield.

Four different radar warning receivers have been installed in the A-10: AN/ALR-46 (aircraft prior to 75-0299); AN/ALR-46A (75-0299 through 76-0554); AN/ALR-64 (77-0177 through 77-0276); and AN/ALR-69 (aircraft 78-0582 and subsequent). Each radar warning system detects the presence of radar emissions, and provides visual and aural indications of threat radar emitters operating in the C/D, and E-J bands. All of the systems provide the capability to detect missile activity and missile launch conditions. The ALR-64 and ALR-69 provide the ability to display the

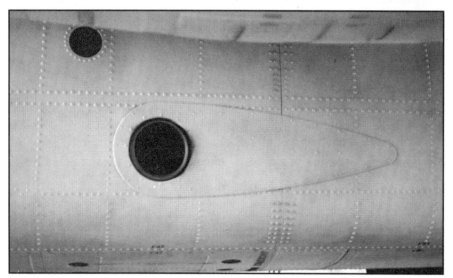

The exhaust port for the auxiliary power unit (APU) is located under the left engine nacelle. The air intake is located on the opposite side. Noteworthy is the use of non-flush rivets, something more common on Russian aircraft than American. Most of the forward fuselage is flush-riveted, but Republic and the Air Force agreed that the adverse aerodynamic affects of using conventional rivets on the rear fuselage were not bad enough to justify the additional cost of the flush rivets. (Dennis R. Jenkins)

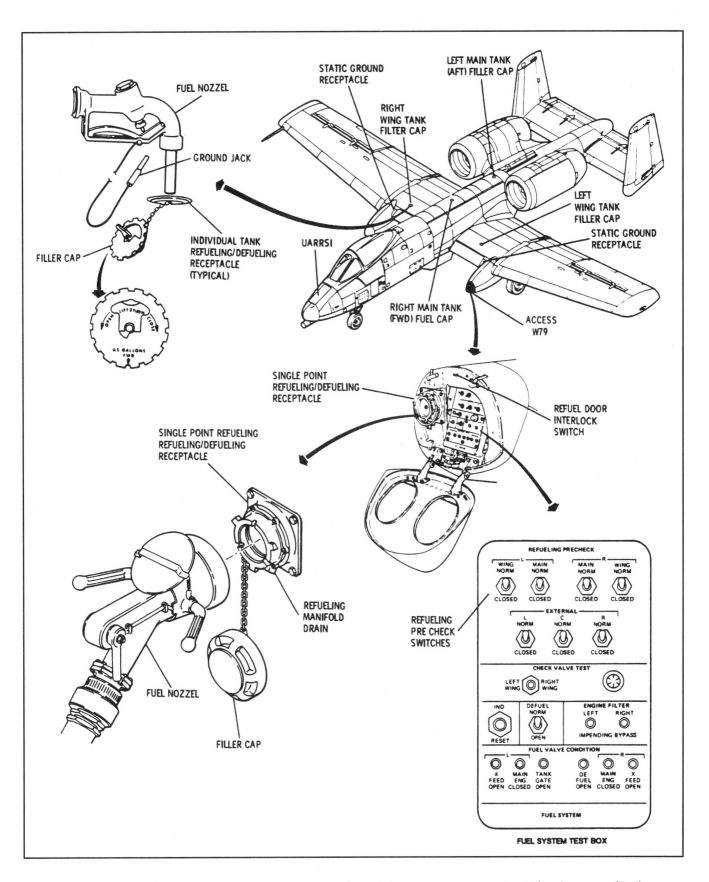

FUEL NOZZEL

GROUND JACK

FILLER CAP

INDIVIDUAL TANK
REFUELING/DEFUELING
RECEPTACLE
(TYPICAL)

STATIC GROUND
RECEPTACLE

RIGHT
WING TANK
FILTER CAP

LEFT MAIN TANK
(AFT) FILLER CAP

LEFT
WING TANK
FILLER CAP

STATIC GROUND
RECEPTACLE

UARRSI

RIGHT MAIN TANK
(FWD) FUEL CAP

ACCESS
W79

OPEN LIFT TURN CLOSE

U.S. GALLONS
FWD

SINGLE POINT
REFUELING/DEFUELING
RECEPTACLE

SINGLE POINT REFUELING
REFUELING/DEFUELING
RECEPTACLE

REFUEL DOOR
INTERLOCK
SWITCH

REFUELING
MANIFOLD
DRAIN

FUEL NOZZEL

FILLER CAP

REFUELING
PRE CHECK
SWITCHES

REFUELING PRECHECK

	L		R	
WING NORM	MAIN NORM		MAIN NORM	WING NORM
CLOSED	CLOSED		CLOSED	CLOSED

EXTERNAL

L			R	
NORM	C NORM		R NORM	
CLOSED	CLOSED		CLOSED	

CHECK VALVE TEST

LEFT WING   RIGHT WING

IND	DEFUEL NORM	ENGINE FILTER	
		LEFT	RIGHT
RESET	OPEN	IMPENDING BYPASS	

FUEL VALVE CONDITION

L				R	
X FEED OPEN	MAIN ENG CLOSED	TANK GATE OPEN	DE FUEL OPEN	MAIN ENG CLOSED	X FEED OPEN

FUEL SYSTEM

FUEL SYSTEM TEST BOX

Single-point refueling is normal for most military aircraft, and the A-10 is no exception. What is unusual is the user-friendly location of the single-point refueling receptacle under a hinged cover on the front of the left main landing gear sponson, complete with all the controls necessary. (U.S. Air Force)

launch quadrant on an azimuth indicator in the cockpit. Various modifications over the years have resulted in all A/OA-10s carrying either the late model ALR-64 or the ALR-69.

Aircraft after 77-0227 were equipped to carry AN/ALE-40 expendable countermeasures dispensers. Earlier aircraft were subsequently modified to the same configuration. A total of 16 MJU-11/A 30-round magazines can be carried, four under each wingtip and four in the back of each landing gear sponson. The color coding on the bottom of each cartridge differentiates flares from chaff—flares carry an "F" placarded on a red end cap, while chaff have brown end caps.

Shortly after Bell laboratories demonstrated the first laser in 1964 the military began to deploy laser designator systems for precision-guided munitions in Vietnam. Airborne laser designators, such as PAVE KNIFE and PAVE TACK were very expensive, so a simple laser receiver was developed under project PAVE PENNY for the A-7, A-10, and F-16, although the F-16 never carried the system operationally. The AN/AAS-35(V) Target Identification Set, Laser (TISL) is carried by the A-10A on a pylon on the front right side of the forward fuselage. The TISL is not a laser designator, but is a laser receiver that senses coded energy pulses reflected from targets designated by other aircraft or ground troops. It then projects a symbol on the HUD to help the pilot locate his target more quickly. PAVE PENNY has demonstrated the ability to detect reflected laser energy as far away as five miles. The PAVE PENNY pod is a very economical device, costing only $217,471.

The A-10 is equipped with an auxiliary power unit (APU) to eliminate the need for externally assisted starting, and to allow systems to be run-up or checked without starting the engines. The APU's intake is located on the right side of the aircraft, underneath the engine, with the exhaust on the opposite side, where it generally leaves a stain on the bottom of the left engine nacelle.

In order to meet the endurance specifications, the A-10 is powered by two 9,065 lbf General Electric TF34-GE-100A high-bypass turbofan engines. The bypass air from the turbofan engine also cools the exhaust plume, reducing the A-10's vulnerability to IR missiles. To fur-

Even though the A-10 is a very simple aircraft, without a great deal of avionics, it still has a fair number of antennas. This particular drawing is prior to the LASTE and ALR-69 upgrades, which added yet more antennas (the most obvious being the two antennas on the side of each vertical stabilizer). (U.S. Air Force)

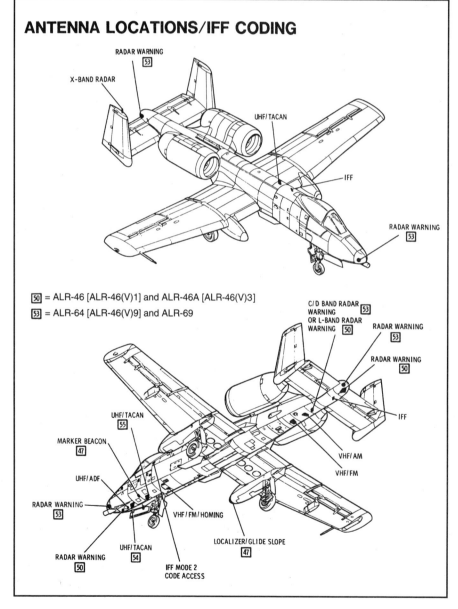

ANTENNA LOCATIONS/IFF CODING

RADAR WARNING 53

X-BAND RADAR

UHF/TACAN

IFF

RADAR WARNING 53

50 = ALR-46 [ALR-46(V)1] and ALR-46A [ALR-46(V)3]
53 = ALR-64 [ALR-46(V)9] and ALR-69

C/D BAND RADAR WARNING 53
OR L-BAND RADAR WARNING 50

RADAR WARNING 53

RADAR WARNING 50

IFF

VHF/AM

VHF/FM

UHF/TACAN 55

MARKER BEACON 47

UHF/ADF

RADAR WARNING 53

VHF/FM/HOMING

LOCALIZER/GLIDE SLOPE 47

UHF/TACAN 54

IFF MODE 2 CODE ACCESS

RADAR WARNING 50

All operational A-10s carry ALE-40 expendable countermeasures dispensers under the wingtips and in the rear of each landing gear sponson. (Don Logan)

During Desert Storm, A-10As expended 355,381 bundles of chaff and 108,654 flares in self-defense, an average of over 40 bundles of chaff and 12 flares per sortie. (U.S. Air Force)

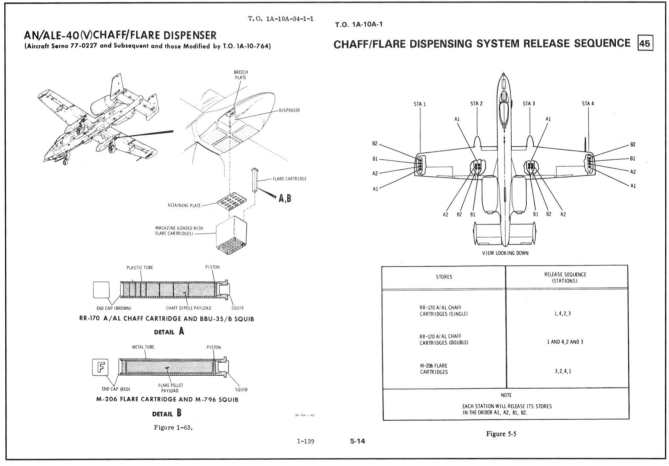

Figure 1-63.

Figure 5-5

ther reduce the threat from sur-face-launched IR missiles, the engines are positioned high on the aft fuselage, just ahead of and above the empennage. This config-uration forms a "box" which hides the exhaust gases for several more feet, allowing additional time for the gases to cool before becoming visible from the ground. The only major drawback to the turbofan engines is the A-10's combination of large frontal area (i.e., drag) and the slow spoolup time of the engines results in relatively poor acceleration. This lack of accelera-tion has been a matter of some concern to the pilots, making it particularly hard to avoid missile attacks at low level during weapons delivery. The pilots tend to push the throttles forward during bomb runs, and frequently this engine spool-up is accompanied by deploying the speedbrakes to maintain proper airspeed. This has significantly increased the maintenance necessary on the engines, but it is a reasonable price to pay for the additional safety it provides the pilots.

The A-10 has a never-to-exceed speed of 518 mph, and a maximum "clean" speed at sea level of 439 mph. Normal cruising speed at sea level is 345 mph. Using three external tanks the aircraft has a ferry range of 2,454 miles. A clean aircraft has a maximum rate of climb of 6,000 feet per minute at sea level. The basic aircraft has an empty weight of 21,541 pounds, with a maximum take-off weight of 50,000 pounds.

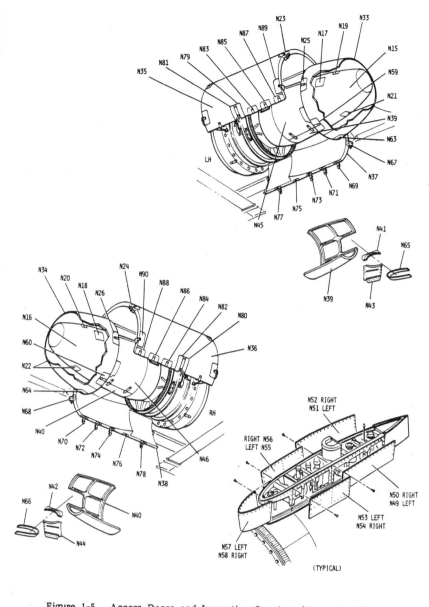

Figure 1-5. Access Doors and Inspection Openings (Sheet 5 of 5)

The location of the TF34 engines makes access to them comparatively easy. It is normal to see an aluminum ladder, the type you can buy in any hardware store, next to each A-10. (U.S. Air Force)

Despite hopes to the contrary, the TF34 is only used by the A-10 and the Navy's S-3. Both aircraft are scheduled to remain in service for the foreseeable future. (Mick Roth)

The ever-present aluminum ladders provide access to most A-10 maintenance locations. Somewhat unusually, a pilot access ladder is positioned on the side of the fuselage instead of using the built-in access ladder. (Ken Kubik via Ken Neubeck)

The AAS-35(V) target identification set, laser (TISL), better known as PAVE PENNY, is carried on a stub pylon on the right front fuselage. (Mike Campbell via the Mick Roth Collection)

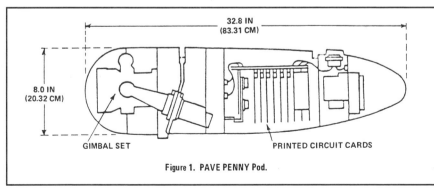

8.0 IN
(20.32 CM)

32.8 IN
(83.31 CM)

GIMBAL SET

PRINTED CIRCUIT CARDS

Figure 1. PAVE PENNY Pod.

PAVE PENNY is a simple laser receiver. Unlike the much more sophisticated LANTIRN pods carried by the F-15E and F-16, the AAS-35 can not designate targets. That job goes to another aircraft, or more likely ground troops. PAVE PENNY does present symbology on the HUD to help guide the A-10 pilot to the target. (U.S. Air Force)

COLD WAR 'HOGS

The A-10 was always intended for use in Europe, and the first aircraft were delivered to the USAFE's 81st TFW during January 1979. The Connecticut ANG became the first Guard user of the aircraft that April (and also the first Guard unit to receive a fighter not "handed down" by the regulars), while the Reservists at Barksdale became the first AFRES recipients of the type in June. A-10As were also sent to PACAF and Alaska in November and December 1981, respectively.

European operations for the A-10 were centered around the main operating bases (MOB) at RAF Bentwaters and RAF Woodbridge in England, supporting several forward operating locations (FOL) in Germany. Small detachments of A-10s rotated through the FOLs on a continual basis, allowing pilots to become familiar with the units they would have to defend, as well as the terrain in the most probable areas of Soviet attack. Over time, many pilots actually became able to work their 60 by 15 mile sectors

of responsibility without referencing topographical maps. Although the focus was Germany, A-10As were also prepared to deploy in support of other NATO allies, such as Norway and Italy.

There were six FOLs, three under the control of each Allied Tactical Air Force (ATAF) in Germany. Only four FOLs had active squadrons (Ahlhorn, Leipheim, Noervenich, and Sembach), while the other two (Jever and Wiesbaden) would have been activated only in the event of

The A-10s were painted in standard European One camouflage for their duty in Europe, replacing the MASK 10A paint used by the units at Davis Monthan during early operations. A-10s almost always carry an ECM pod on one of the outer wing stations. This A-10 is carrying an ALQ-119(V) pod, although Warthogs operating in Europe generally carried one of the ALQ-131 variants. (Kevin L. Patrick via the Mick Roth Collection)

The Fighter Weapons School at Nellis AFB near Las Vegas was amongst the first operators of the A-10, and continues to operate a small number of the type for tactics development and training.
(Mick Roth Collection)

The four forward operating locations in western Germany were all well within the A-10's range of East Germany and expected entry points for Soviet forces.
(U.S. Air Force)

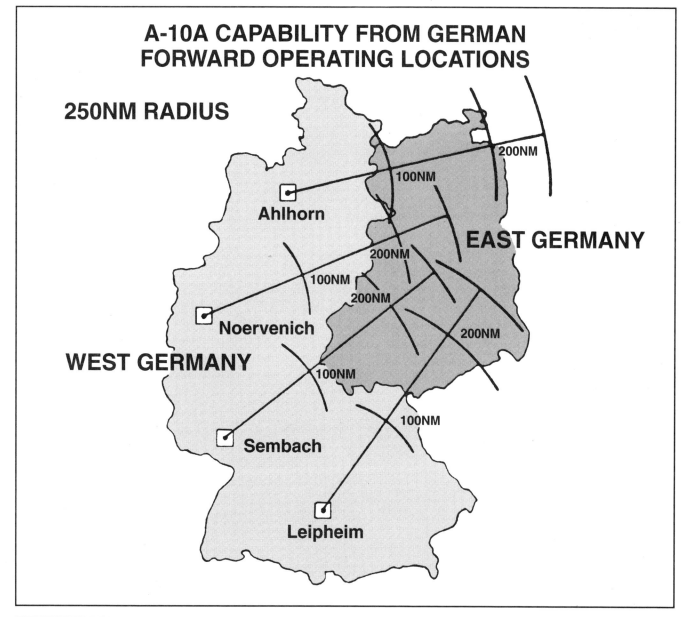

A-10A CAPABILITY FROM GERMAN FORWARD OPERATING LOCATIONS

250NM RADIUS

200NM

100NM

EAST GERMANY

Ahlhorn

200NM

100NM

200NM

Noervenich

200NM

WEST GERMANY

100NM

100NM

Sembach

Leipheim

Flying the A-10 on ferry missions was not an easy task for most of the aircraft's life. The lack of an autopilot forced the pilot to remain awake and alert for prolonged periods of time. The lack of an inertial navigation system in early aircraft meant that flights of A-10s had to rely upon navigation assistance from nearby tankers during overwater flights. And the A-10's maximum speed was very close to the stall speed of the KC-135 tankers, making aerial refueling challenging. The addition of an INS and autopilot, and soon a global positioning system receiver, have made this process much easier in recent years. (U.S. Air Force)

war. Although the FOLs were capable of minor maintenance and emergency repairs, aircraft returned to the UK for major maintenance. Contingency plans accounted for the loss of the usual runways at the FOLs, and the A-10s could have used the undamaged part of the runway or a taxiway, or even deployed to emergency airstrips using straight sections of autobahn. In fact, on several occasions A-10As were allowed to practice on new stretches of the roadway before they were opened to the public for automobile traffic.

Each squadron was assigned to a specific FOL, but the two squadrons assigned to the contingency locations rotated through the other

The amount of contrast between the various colors of the European One camouflage is unusual. Also noteworthy, the wingtip speedbrakes are open, and the aircraft is fitted with a Battelle gun gas diverter. A PAVE PENNY pod is fitted to the stub pylon on the forward fuselage. For most of the A-10's career the PAVE PENNY pod was painted grey. (Bob Niedermeier via the Mick Roth Collection)

The AGM-65 Maverick has proven to be one of the A-10's most effective weapon. There are four Air Force versions of Maverick: AGM-65A/B television-guided missiles; AGM-65D IIR-guided missiles; and AGM-65G IIR-guided missiles. The A/B and D versions were equipped with 125-pound shaped charge warheads for use against armor, while the G models were equipped with 300-pound kinetic penetrator warheads for use against high-value targets such as bunkers, locomotives, sheltered aircraft, and SAM sites. (U.S. Air Force)

FOLs one week out of three. This arrangement resulted in each squadron having eight of its aircraft deployed two weeks out of three, keeping 32 A-10As in Germany at all times. A normal pilot rotation was two weeks at the FOL, flying twice a day, followed by four weeks in England, flying about twice a week. NATO planning in the event of war depended heavily on reinforcements arriving from the U.S. to sustain the war effort, and pilots from U.S. A-10 units periodically traveled to Europe as part of operation BOAR SWAP to improve their knowledge of flying conditions, terrain, and procedures. This allowed a frequent exchange of information without the time and expense of deploying entire squadrons and their aircraft.

If the Cold War had ever turned hot, 18 aircraft would have deployed to each FOL, including the two contingency locations. During combat operations, three two-ship formations from each FOL would have been in contact with Warsaw Pact forces, with six more aircraft en route to the battle, while the remaining six aircraft would have been on the ground being refueled and rearmed. Coordination between ground forces and the A-10As would have been provided by OV-10A Bronco forward

A variety of scoops, antennas, and the fuel vent present a bizarre appearance under the rear fuselage. (Mick Roth)

RADAR WARNING SYSTEM

1. ON AIRCRAFT PRIOR TO SERNO 76-0533 AND AIRCRAFT NOT MODIFIED BY T.O. 1A-10-684.
2. ON AIRCRAFT SERNO 76-0533 AND SUBSEQUENT AND AIRCRAFT MODIFIED BY T.O. 1A-10-684.
3. ALL CENTER LEGENDS OF SWITCH-INDICATORS WILL COME ON WHEN SYSTEM IS TURNED ON.

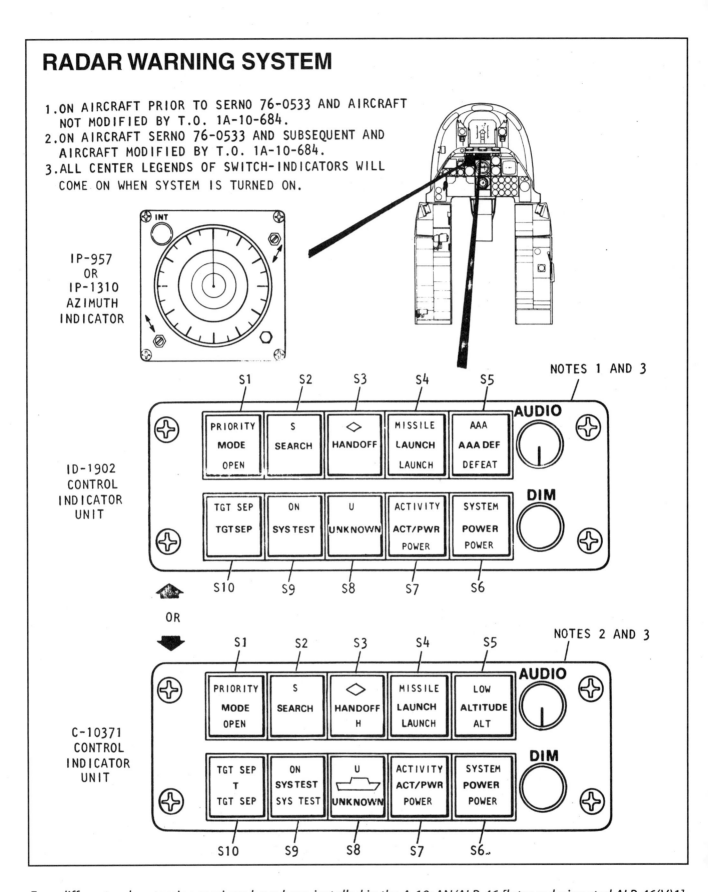

Four different radar warning receivers have been installed in the A-10: AN/ALR-46 [later redesignated ALR-46(V)1]; AN/ALR-46A [ALR-46(V)3]; AN/ALR-64 [ALR-46(V)9]; and AN/ALR-69. Currently most aircraft have the AN/ALR-69(V) system installed. (U.S. Air Force)

The OA-10A would eventually replace the North American Rockwell OV-10A Bronco as a forward air control (FAC) aircraft. However, when this photo was taken in the late 1970s, they were envisioned as operating as a team in support of ground forces. (U.S. Air Force)

air controllers (FAC) operating just behind the battle line. Air liaison officers, Air Force pilots operating with the Army ground units, would have relayed information to the FACs, who would pass it on to the A-10s and Army attack helicopters.

Each wingtip contains a large speedbrake that is also used as an aileron. Note that the trim-tab is attached to the upper speedbrake surface (and the corresponding cut-out in the lower surface). Early in the A-10's career the insides of the speedbrakes were painted bright red, but later this gave way to green or grey, depending upon the general paint scheme of the aircraft. (Don Logan)

The prototypes did not include an integrated boarding ladder, making access to the cockpit difficult (and requiring an additional piece of support equipment). All production aircraft had an integrated boarding ladder, shown here in its fully deployed position. (Bruce Stewart via the Mick Roth Collection)

Tactics developed during the earlier JAWS exercises were refined and renamed joint air attack team (JAAT) operations. The A-10As would attack a Warsaw-Pact armored column from just above 100 feet, hitting its AAA and SAM defenses with Mavericks, before dropping behind terrain for cover. With the defenses suppressed, Army attack helicopters would prosecute the tanks from less than 100 feet with TOW and Hellfire antitank missiles and cannon fire, taking turns with the reattacking A-10As. The helicopters would also cover the A-10A's departure before heading for home themselves.

The lack of formation light strips on the forward fuselage, wingtips, and vertical stabilizers indicates this aircraft has not received the night vision modifications that were performed in the 1990s. (Mick Roth Collection)

This A-10 from Osan AB, South Korea, is carrying a Maverick training round, evidenced by the lack of control fins on the rear of the missile. (Mick Roth Collection)

Although the FAC played an important part in combat operations, the Vietnam-vintage OA-37Bs and OV-10As. The Air Force was also seeking ways to continue justifying the purchase of additional F-15 and F-16 fighters. Part of this justification including declaring the A-10A obsolete, and assigning modified F-16s to the CAS role. This allowed the Air Force to reassign some of the redesignated OA-10s to the FAC mission beginning in late 1987. There is no physical difference between a standard A-10 and an OA-10. It is interesting to note the increasingly politicized and bizarre way in which American combat aircraft are designated; F-16s with different engine/inlet combinations and primary missions (day versus night attack with LANTIRN) are all called F-l6C/Ds, while the OA-10A received a completely new designation because of a mission change even though no physical changes were amde to the aircraft.

The external fuel tanks carried by the A-10 were not only identical to those used by the FB-111A, in many cases they were the same tanks, explaining the dark green paint on these. (Ben Knowles via the Mick Roth Collection)

DEPLETED URANIUM

AND OTHER THINGS THAT GO BOOM

The A-10 is built around a single 679-pound 30mm General Electric GAU-8/A Avenger cannon. The bulk of the weapon is offset slightly to the left so that the firing barrel is always on the centerline, depressed 2°from the aircraft's waterline. The GAU-8/A is actually the firing part of the A/A49E-6 weapons system which weighs 4,200 pounds, including a drum that normally contains 1,174 rounds of 30mm ammunition. The whole unit is about the same size and weight as a family car, and was frequently shown dwarfing a Volkswagen Beetle in the early years of service. The cannon muzzle protrudes from the fuselage nose with the cannon mechanism located under the cockpit and the ammunition drum located in the area just behind the cockpit. Two selectable firing rates are available, 2,100 (±200) or 4,200 (+200/-600) rounds per minute. In 1987 the maximum rate was temporarily reduced to 3,900 rpm in preparation for the Battelle gun gas diverter modification which was later cancelled. Since most bursts are only a few seconds long, it is more practical to think in terms of 35 and 65 rounds per second.

Like other modern Gatling-type weapons, it takes a short while for the cannon to begin rotating at full speed, and "only" 50 rounds are expended during the first second of operation. Spent cases are retained within the ammunition drum, and are not discarded. Loading requires a specialized piece of ground support equipment, the only such equipment needed by the A-10, and can simultaneously unload spent cases and reload new ones, accomplishing a complete change in just 13 minutes with only a single technician. (text continued on page 69)

The wild "warthog" face is one of the more interesting pieces of nose art to adorn the A-10. Almost all 917th Wing aircraft have carried some variation of this face, and other units occasionally use similar art. Gives new meaning to the term "Go Ugly early," which generally refers to troops calling in A-10 support early in a battle. (William D. Spidle via the Mick Roth Collection)

WARBIRD**TECH**
SERIES

GO UGLY EARLY

The A-10 has only had three primary color schemes: the early MASK 10A grey scheme that was used by the first sixteen operational aircraft, the dark European One paint scheme used during the cold war, and the newest two-tone grey scheme used after Desert Storm.

But along the way there have been several interesting diversions. The aircraft that participated in the JAWS exercises wore very unusual "spotted" camouflage, while each of the DT&E aircraft carried a differ-

The first 16 A-10s used the MASK 10A asymmetrical paint scheme. Noteworthy is that the closest aircraft has not yet received its "DM" tailcodes. (U.S. Air Force)

Each of the A-10As used in the JAWS exercises used a different version of this "spotted" camouflage, but none were adopted for operational use. (Mick Roth)

ent paint scheme for evaluation.

And although not presented in any detail here, the A-10s used in Desert Storm frequently sported some very interesting nose art (although not all of it was on the nose). Interested readers should pick up a copy of Don Logan's excellent photo book on the A-10.

One of the most urgent problems that surfaced during early testing was unburned propellant being expelled with the gun gases. The unburned propellant usually ignited, causing a brilliant fireball to erupt around the nose of the A-10. A change in the propellant chemistry solved the fireball problem, but gun gas ingestion remains a problem with the A-10. Noteworthy is the shield built-up around the gun muzzle on the first prototype YA-10. (U.S. Air Force)

This is how the A-10 looks in 1998. Two-tone grey paint, formation light strips on the forward fuselage, wingtips, and vertical stabilizer, and ALR-69(V) radar warning antennas on the nose. Barely visible is part of the "false canopy" on the nose landing gear door. (Charles E. Stewart via the Mick Roth Collection)

A couple of different DT&E aircraft had their wingtips and rudders painted dayglo orange to improve visibility during test flights. This was the climate test aircraft which had a mottled white over black base coat camouflage pattern. (Dennis R. Jenkins via the Mick Roth Collection)

The 917th TFW at Barksdale AFB tested two experimental paint schemes during 1991. This is "Peanut," a mostly brown scheme meant for desert areas. A similar grey scheme was known as "Flipper," but neither were adopted. (U.S. Air Force)

A couple of triple ejector racks (TER) hang under the inner wing stations on this European One paint scheme A-10. Weapons and their racks frequently do not match the color scheme of the rest of the aircraft, greatly reducing the effectiveness of the carefully studied camouflage pattern.
(Mick Roth Collection)

An A-10A from the 74th FS, 23rd FG, taking off from Ahmed Al-Jaber Air Base, Kuwait, on 12 March 1998, for a combat patrol mission over Iraq. A-10's of the 74th have been flying since 1994 in support of Operation Southern Watch.
(A1C Greg L. Davis, U.S. Air Force)

A lucky pilot. The damage to the A-10's rear fuselage is visible in the background, as is the obvious wheels-up landing. This A-10 would not fly again, being stripped of all useful parts and buried in the desert instead of being returned to the United States. (MSgt Patrick J. McGee)

For most of its career, this was the A-10's cockpit. The three fire extinguisher handles are visible on the edge of the cowl—the middle one is for the APU, while the outer ones are for the engine on that side. The radar warning receiver indicators and directional scope are at the top center and slightly left. The TV monitor on the right is used to target and guide the Maverick missiles. (Mick Roth)

Some of the Desert Storm nose art was very elaborate. Here is the "Night Penetrator". Noteworthy are the kill marks in white halfway back on the fuselage. A JP-4/8 recycle drum is on the ground under the fuselage. (J. E. Michaels via the Mick Roth Collection)

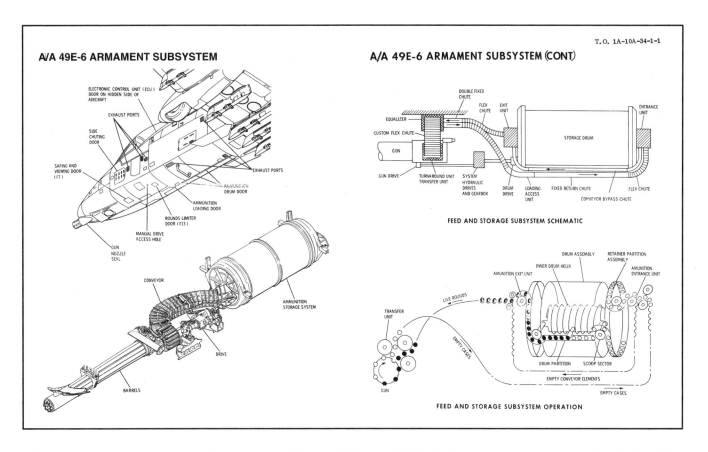

A/A 49E-6 ARMAMENT SUBSYSTEM

A/A 49E-6 ARMAMENT SUBSYSTEM (CONT)

FEED AND STORAGE SUBSYSTEM SCHEMATIC

FEED AND STORAGE SUBSYSTEM OPERATION

The A-10 is built around a single 679-pound General Electric GAU-8/A Avenger 30mm cannon. The bulk of the weapon is offset slightly to the left of the aircraft so that the firing barrel is always on the centerline. The GAU-8/A is actually the firing part of the A/A49E-6 weapons system which weighs 4,200 pounds, including a drum that normally contains 1,174 rounds of 30mm ammunition. (U.S. Air Force)

(text continued from page 64)

The cannon is driven by a gearbox with two separately controlled hydraulic drive motors and control valves mounted on the support structure between the cannon and ammunition storage system. The entire gun system is installed using six bolts, two at the mid-barrel location and four at the aft of the gun housing. Electrical power is required from at least one aircraft generator or the auxiliary power unit (APU). Both hydraulic systems are required to fire at the high rate, but low rate operation can be sustained with only one hydraulic system operational. The GAU-8/A is bore-sighted to 41 mils below the zero sight line, and is optimized for 4,000 feet slant range while the aircraft is in a 30° dive at 250 knots KIAS. A counter on the cockpit armament panels displays the number of rounds remaining in 10-round decrements.

The GAU-8/A has two selectable firing rates available, 2,100 (±200) or 4,200 (+200/-600) rounds per minute. In 1987 the maximum rate was temporarily reduced to 3,900 rpm in preparation for the Battelle gun gas diverter modification which was later cancelled. (U.S. Air Force)

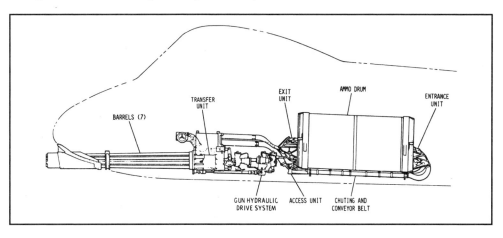

The only piece of specialized ground equipment needed by the A-10 is this ammunition loader. The unit can simultaneously unload spent cases and reload new ones, changing a full load in 13 minutes. (Cradle of Aviation Museum via Ken Neubeck)

The A-10 cannon and HUD are boresighted by placing the aircraft on jacks and leveling the aircraft. A sight board is placed 1,036.9 inches (86 feet, 4.9 inches) in front of the aircraft at a predetermined height. A special visible laser device is placed into the front of the barrel that is in the firing position. Its location is then noted on the sight board. The cannon is rotated, and the procedure repeated for each barrel. This ensures all barrels are generally aligned with each other. If one is found out of alignment, the cannon is pulled and the condition corrected. The HUD is then aligned using the location marked on the board from the gun alignment process. This ensures the HUD and gun are aligned with each other.

The most common load is called a "combat mix" (CM) and consists of a single 1.47-pound PGU-13/B high-

The amount of gun gas produced by the GAU-8/A is enormous, and has presented more than its share of problems with gun gas ingestion. This photo clearly shows the problem—note the cloud of gun gas streaming into the engines. The size of the 2,000 pound laser guided bomb under the right wing is evident. (U.S. Air Force)

explosive incendiary (HEI) round mixed in with five 1.635-pound PGU-14A/B armor-piercing incendiary (API) rounds. The depleted uranium (DU) projectile from the PGU-14 weighs 0.94 pounds and leaves the barrel traveling 3,240 feet per second. This round can kill most main battle tanks from as far away as 21,600 feet. The projectile is specifically designed to have enough energy to penetrate tank armor; once inside the tank, it stays there in a mostly molten state. The API round has proven effective

The size of the 30mm cannon was high publicized during the early part of the program, and this photo was the one that showed up in many magazines. The cannon is driven by a gearbox with two separately controlled hydraulic drive motors. (Fairchild-Republic)

even against "reactive" armor used by Russian tanks, and also against the newest DU armor. The HEI rounds provide a visual reference for the pilot, much like tracers used to. There is a low-cost PGU-15/B target practice (TP) round available that has also proven to be useful against lightly armored vehicle. All projectiles use an aluminum cartridge case for lightness and have plastic instead of copper bands on the shell itself. These save weight and cost, and save wear on the barrel, extending life and acting as crude barrel cleaners. The Air Force specified a minimum barrel life of 21,000 rounds. Over 80 million rounds of 30mm ammunition have been manufactured by Honeywell and Aerojet. All of these rounds use Hercules-25 (HC-25) propellant.

Most A-10 strikes are conducted from between 5,000 and 15,000 feet slant-range (SR) from the target. At 10,000 feet it takes a round 4.56 seconds to reach the target. This flight time increases to 9.79 seconds at 15,000 feet. The pilot must tell the computer what type of ammunition (API, HEI, or TP) he is firing. Although there are two ammunition manufacturers, the LASTE ballistic computer uses the ballistic characteristics of the Honeywell rounds in its computations. At slant ranges up to 12,000 feet, the LASTE algorithms are accurate to within one milliradian (mil) of actual. It should be noted that for combat mix there is an appreciable difference in the drift between API and HEI rounds because the API round is more aerodynamic. With the CM algorithm selected, at 12,000 feet SR the API rounds will impact the target, but the HEI rounds will fall 5.36 mils short and 1.6 mils to the right. At 15,000 feet the API rounds will impact 1.18 mils short, while the HEI rounds will impact 14 mils short and 2.6 mils to the right. In both cases, the HEI rounds impact approximately one second after the API rounds due to their different aerodynamics.

During Operation Desert Storm, 940,254 rounds of combat mix were fired, for an average of 119 rounds per sortie, just a two-second burst. An additional 16,360 rounds of HEI were fired by OA-10As from the 23rd TASS, which did not use combat mix, an average of only 18 per sortie. The GAU-8/A proved so deadly to Iraqi tanks that the pilots soon began referring to "plinking

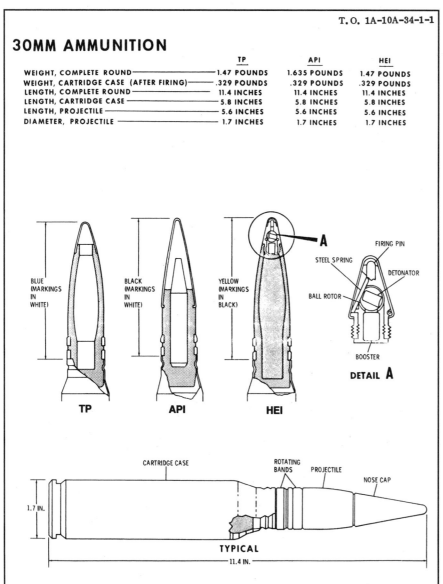

30MM AMMUNITION

	TP	API	HEI
WEIGHT, COMPLETE ROUND	1.47 POUNDS	1.635 POUNDS	1.47 POUNDS
WEIGHT, CARTRIDGE CASE (AFTER FIRING)	.329 POUNDS	.329 POUNDS	.329 POUNDS
LENGTH, COMPLETE ROUND	11.4 INCHES	11.4 INCHES	11.4 INCHES
LENGTH, CARTRIDGE CASE	5.8 INCHES	5.8 INCHES	5.8 INCHES
LENGTH, PROJECTILE	5.6 INCHES	5.6 INCHES	5.6 INCHES
DIAMETER, PROJECTILE	1.7 INCHES	1.7 INCHES	1.7 INCHES

BLUE (MARKINGS IN WHITE)

BLACK (MARKINGS IN WHITE)

YELLOW (MARKINGS IN BLACK)

FIRING PIN
STEEL SPRING
DETONATOR
BALL ROTOR
BOOSTER

DETAIL A

TP   API   HEI

CARTRIDGE CASE   ROTATING BANDS   PROJECTILE   NOSE CAP

1.7 IN.

TYPICAL
11.4 IN.

The most common ammunition load is called a "combat mix" (CM) and consists of a single 1.5-pound PGU-13/B HEI round mixed in with five 1.65-pound PGU-14A/B API rounds. There is a low-cost PGU-15/B target practice (TP) round available that has also proven to be useful against lightly armored vehicles. Over 80 million rounds of 30mm ammunition have been manufactured by Honeywell and Aerojet. All of these rounds use Hercules-25 (HC-25) propellant. (U.S. Air Force)

The armament controls are, like the rest of the A-10, very simple by modern standards. The armament control panel (below) is shown as it was originally installed before the AIM-9 Sidewinder controls were added (the new panel is shown later). A simple four-digit counter shows the pilot the number of 30mm rounds remaining. Each of the 11 weapons stations is wired for up to four weapons, although three is the maximum that are normally carried. (U.S. Air Force)

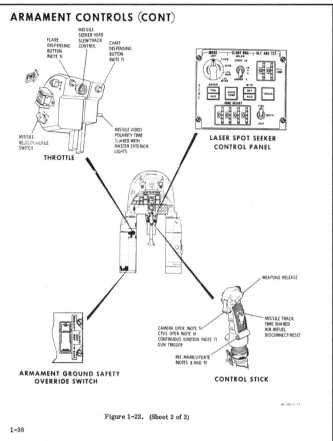

ARMAMENT CONTROLS (CONT)

LASER SPOT SEEKER CONTROL PANEL

THROTTLE

ARMAMENT GROUND SAFETY OVERRIDE SWITCH

CONTROL STICK

Figure 1-22. (Sheet 2 of 2)

1-38

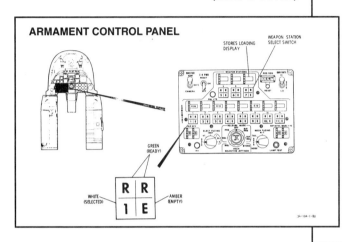

ARMAMENT CONTROL PANEL

tanks." Velocity is the dominant factor for penetration of the API round. At 15,000 feet slant-range, the API round has a velocity of 900 feet per second and can penetrate 0.2 inches of rolled homogeneous armor (RHA). At 2,000 feet SR, the velocity is 3,400 feet per second and the round can penetrate 3.02 inches of RHA, while at 10,000 feet SR the velocity is 1,300 feet per second with 0.8 inches of penetration. The API round is designed to defeat armored vehicles, and is not particularly effective against light-skinned targets such as trucks and aircraft since it tends to just punch holes in them and not explode.

Against light-skinned targets, the HEI round has demonstrated the capability to penetrate 0.25 inches of mild steel or thick aluminum at an impact velocity of approximately 900 feet per second. At 15,000

feet SR, the impact velocity of an HEI round is 850 feet per second. Even if an HEI round falls short, it causes considerable fragmentation damage if it strikes within two feet of a soft vehicle. These high velocity HEI fragments will most probably penetrate the target's skin, severing fuel and electrical lines, killing the crew, and producing major structural damage. The HEI round can also ignite flammable objects within 16 feet, and has the ability to create secondary fires that may engulf the vehicle.

The latest LASTE software has produced a considerably improved probability of hitting the target. For example, shooting a beam shot at an Mi-24 helicopter at 12,000 feet SR, a one second burst at high rate will result in 15 rounds hitting the target. At 15,000 feet SR, the hit rate drops to 4 rounds.

The DU used by the 30mm API rounds has received a great deal of coverage in the popular press after the Gulf War. Depleted uranium is the material that remains after the "useful" U-235 isotope is removed from natural uranium. The U-235 isotope can be used in nuclear weapons or as fuel for nuclear reactors, but makes up less than 1% of naturally occurring uranium. Fifty years of processing ore to obtain weapons-grade material and nuclear fuel has left the U.S. with over one billion pounds of DU. During the early 1970s, the U.S. began investigating potential uses for the rapidly accumulating DU stockpiles. Depleted uranium has several properties that make it ideal for military applications. It is extremely dense—over 18 times as heavy as water, 3 times steel, and 1.7 times lead. Its surface also ignites on impact, especially with steel.

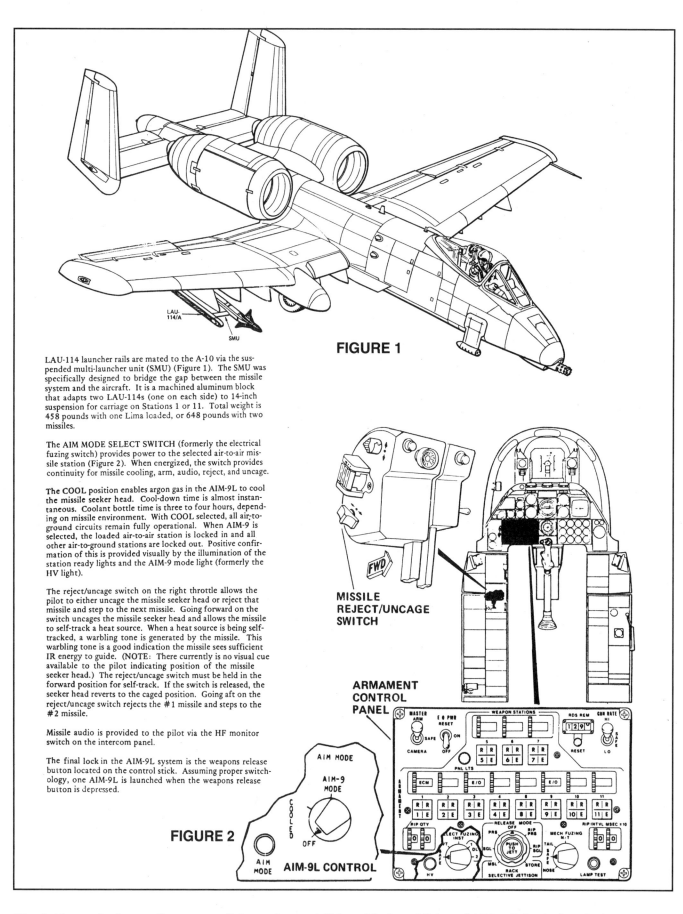

FIGURE 1

LAU-114 launcher rails are mated to the A-10 via the suspended multi-launcher unit (SMU) (Figure 1). The SMU was specifically designed to bridge the gap between the missile system and the aircraft. It is a machined aluminum block that adapts two LAU-114s (one on each side) to 14-inch suspension for carriage on Stations 1 or 11. Total weight is 458 pounds with one Lima loaded, or 648 pounds with two missiles.

The AIM MODE SELECT SWITCH (formerly the electrical fuzing switch) provides power to the selected air-to-air missile station (Figure 2). When energized, the switch provides continuity for missile cooling, arm, audio, reject, and uncage.

The COOL position enables argon gas in the AIM-9L to cool the missile seeker head. Cool-down time is almost instantaneous. Coolant bottle time is three to four hours, depending on missile environment. With COOL selected, all air-to-ground circuits remain fully operational. When AIM-9 is selected, the loaded air-to-air station is locked in and all other air-to-ground stations are locked out. Positive confirmation of this is provided visually by the illumination of the station ready lights and the AIM-9 mode light (formerly the HV light).

The reject/uncage switch on the right throttle allows the pilot to either uncage the missile seeker head or reject that missile and step to the next missile. Going forward on the switch uncages the missile seeker head and allows the missile to self-track a heat source. When a heat source is being self-tracked, a warbling tone is generated by the missile. This warbling tone is a good indication the missile sees sufficient IR energy to guide. (NOTE: There currently is no visual cue available to the pilot indicating position of the missile seeker head.) The reject/uncage switch must be held in the forward position for self-track. If the switch is released, the seeker head reverts to the caged position. Going aft on the reject/uncage switch rejects the #1 missile and steps to the #2 missile.

Missile audio is provided to the pilot via the HF monitor switch on the intercom panel.

The final lock in the AIM-9L system is the weapons release button located on the control stick. Assuming proper switchology, one AIM-9L is launched when the weapons release button is depressed.

MISSILE REJECT/UNCAGE SWITCH

ARMAMENT CONTROL PANEL

FIGURE 2

AIM-9L CONTROL

The A-10 acquired a small measure of air-to-air capabilities with the addition of AIM-9 Sidewinders. (U.S. Air Force)

Various versions of the AGM-65 Maverick can be carried by the A-10 as illustrated by the table at right. (U.S. Air Force)

The Fighter Weapons School at Nellis AFB operates a couple of each fighter type in the inventory. Here a 422nd FWS aircraft fires an AGM-65B during tests. (U.S. Air Force)

GUIDANCE	DESIGNATION	COMMON AIRFRAME AND SUBSYSTEM	WARHEAD	GUIDANCE TECHNOLOGY	ONE DISPLAY = 4 PRESENTATIONS	REMARKS
TV	AGM-65A			● TV 5° FOV ● CENTROID/CONTRAST TRACKER	REAL-TIME TV	● LAUNCH AND LEAVE DAYTIME ATTACK ● MULTIPLE LAUNCHES PER PASS
	AGM-65B		● SHAPED-CHARGED JET AND BLAST ● 125 LBS	● TV'S 2.5° FOV IMPROVED CENTROID/CONTRAST TRACKER	REAL-TIME TV	● SAME AS ABOVE PLUS MAGNIFIED SCENE FOR LONGER TARGET ACQUISITION RANGE
IR	AGM-65D	● AFT/CENTER SECTION ● BOOST-SUSTAIN PROPULSION ● HYDRAULIC SYSTEM		● IMAGING IR ● DUAL FOV	IMAGING-TV DISPLAY	● AUTONOMOUS DAY/NIGHT ATTACK CAPABILITY ● PENETRATES HAZE
	AGM-65F		● KINETIC ENERGY PENETRATOR ● BLAST FRAGMENT ● SELECTABLE FUZE DELAY	● DIGITAL TRACKER		● 65F SOFTWARE OPTIMIZED FOR SHIP ATTACK
	AGM-65G					● 65G SOFTWARE OPTIMIZED FOR USAF MISSION AND SHIP ATTACK
LASER	AGM-65E		● 300 LBS	● PASSIVE LASER ● DIGITAL TRACKER	SYNTHETIC TV DISPLAY	● ATTACKS AGAINST LASER-DESIGNATED TARGETS, DAY AND NIGHT

It has been widely reported that numerous veterans have become ill with Gulf War Syndrome. The DU emits mainly alpha particles, which although they can cause damage to cells and tissue, are easily absorbed by even the most meager of shielding, including clothing. Therefore DU ammunition does not seem to pose an immediate health hazard assuming basic precautions are taken during its handling.

The greatest hazard from DU is the dust formed from impacts or burning. Depleted uranium, basically, oxidizes when exposed to air, turning a dull black color. Impacts or fires can cause DU shrapnel or dust. The main hazard of DU is inhaling the dust, or accidentally picking it up and swallowing it if gloves are not worn and the dust is not washed off prior to eating, drinking, or using the latrine. There has been speculation that some of these veterans may have come in contact with the fine particles of uranium oxide dust generated when a DU penetrator hits armor. The pyrophoric nature of uranium metal is well known, and an estimate used by U.S. Army field commanders is that when a DU penetrator in a cannon round is fired at high velocity against armor, about 10% of it burns up and forms micrometer-size uranium oxide particles that can be inhaled or ingested. However, a report by the Army Environmental Policy Institute (AEPI) describing research on hard target testing states "As much as 70% of a DU penetrator can be aerosolized when it strikes a tank …"

There are of course many differences of opinion concerning the use of DU rounds and it is likely the debate will continue to rage for the foreseeable future. What is relatively certain is that soldiers and civilians in areas where DU ammunition has been used need to be educated about the hazards, and the basic precautions required.

In addition to the CM fired from the A-10s, the U.S. Army reports that "More than 14,000 large caliber (mainly 155mm) DU rounds were consumed during Operations Desert Shield/Desert Storm. As many as 7,000 of these rounds may have been fired in practice. Approximately 4,000 rounds were reportedly fired in combat. The remaining 3,000 rounds are losses that include a substantial loss in a fire at Doha, Kuwait." The 14,000 large caliber rounds contained about 130,000 pounds of DU, in addition to the 783,595 PGU-14 rounds (about 750,000 pounds) fired by the A-10.

In a letter to Senator Sam Nunn, a representative of the U.S. Air Force stated, "… these projectiles are no more hazardous to store, transport, or employ than those composed of lead or copper." This view is echoed in a U.S. Army report to Congress that states, "The health risks associated with using DU in peacetime are minimal. This includes risks associated with transporting, storing and handling intact DU munitions and armor during peacetime."

It should be noted that DU is also used in nonmilitary applications. The flight control counterweights in most modern airliners are made from DU, and a Boeing 747 contains almost 600 pounds of depleted uranium in the aft fuselage.

Despite several in-depth studies there is no conclusive evidence that the use of DU projectiles constitutes a serious public health hazard, unless you happen to be in an enemy tank on the receiving end.

The A-10 is cleared for carriage of most air-to-ground weapons in U.S. inventory, including conventional low-drag and retarded bombs, cluster-bombs, and AGM-65 Maverick missiles. There are 11 non-jettisonable external pylon stations on the aircraft, with #1 at the left wingtip and #11 on the right. Stations 5, 6, and 7 are on the fuselage, with stations 4 and 8 inboard of the main landing gear sponsons. The other stations are outboard of these sponsons. The pylons on stations 2/10 and 5/7 can be removed in high threat areas to improve maneuverability, and this appears to have been done during Operation Desert Storm.

Forward firing munitions, except AIM-9 Sidewinders, may not be carried on stations 1/11, and stores may not be carried on stations 5/7 simultaneously with stores on station 6. The centerline pylon is not wired to accept weapons, and is most often used to carry a 600-gallon fuel tank for ferry operations or a "travel pod" for the pilot's suitcase. Two additional 600-gallon tanks can be carried on stations 4/8.

Mavericks can only be carried on stations 3/9, just outboard of the landing gear sponsons. The primary method of carriage is from single rail LAU-117 launchers, although triple-rail LAU-88s can also be used. When LAU-88s were used during Desert Storm, it was only with slant-loads of two missiles, even though virtually any symmetrical combination is authorized. As of late 1996 there were a total of 9,243 AGM-65A and 5,912 AGM-65B TV Mavericks, 10,400 AGM-65D IIR Mavericks, and 9,055 advanced AGM-65G IIR Mavericks in the U.S. war reserves. All TV Mavericks are now well past their programmed life span, and are beginning to show their age. Roughly 10% of the older missiles that are randomly removed from storage for live-fire tests have defects, usually in their guidance control sections. (Mick Roth Collection)

DIVE BOMB DELIVERY

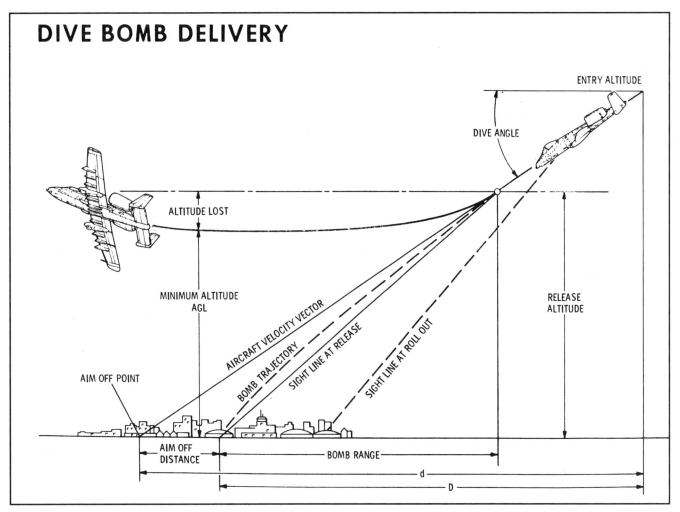

SURFACE ATTACK - GUN

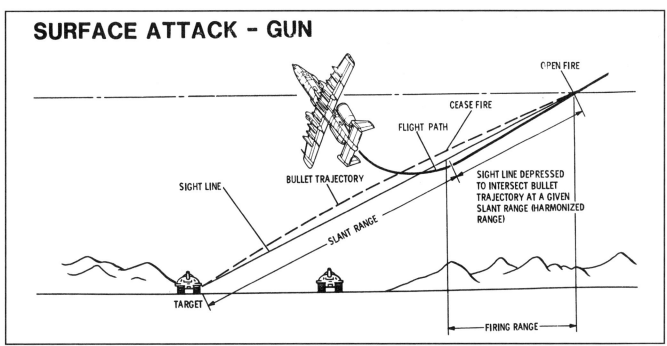

Almost all of the A-10's attack profiles are in fairly steep dives to increase survivability, although the aircraft is fully capable of level bombing, particularly useful when delivering laser guided bombs. (U.S. Air Force)

The A-10 was originally deployed without an air-to-air defensive capability. In December 1981, the 174th TFW from the New York ANG conducted an informal test to add the capability to carry and fire AIM-9 Sidewinders to their A-10 aircraft. The design used existing aircraft wiring and components to the maximum extent possible to minimize cost. By 1983 the Air Force was testing the capability on two aircraft from the 422nd TES at Nellis AFB. A total of 94 test sorties were flown over an 8 month period. The tests ended on 18 November 1983

PAVE PENNY, parent-mounted Mavericks, and rocket pods adorn this LASTE-equipped A-10A. (Charles E. Stewart via the Mick Roth Collection)

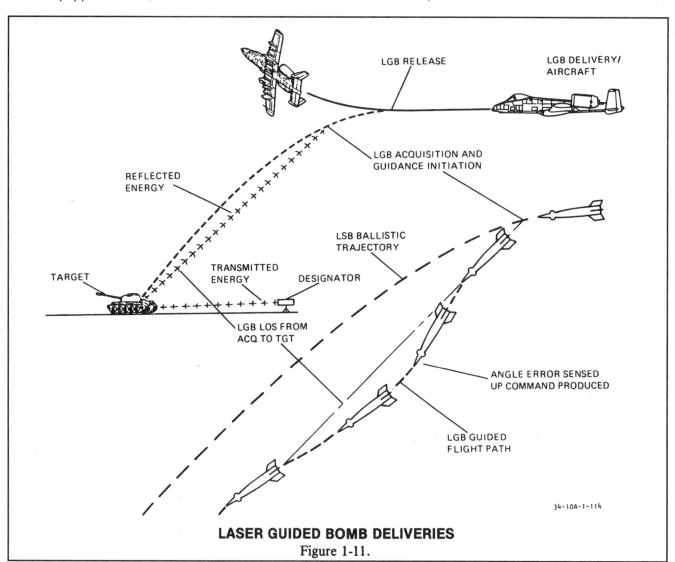

LASER GUIDED BOMB DELIVERIES
Figure 1-11.

The A-10 is capable of dropping laser guided bombs, but unlike the F-15E and some F-16s, can not self-designate targets. Instead, the A-10 pilot relies on ground troops or other aircraft equipped with designators. (U.S. Air Force)

Contrary to popular beliefs, there is nothing particularly special about a laser guided bomb. In fact, any Mk 82/84 "iron" bomb can become laser guided with the addition of a simple field-installed kit consisting of the laser seeker and four control fins. The addition of this kit turns the bombs into either GBU-10 (2,000-pound) or GBU-12 (500-pound) LGBs. (U.S. Air Force)

GBU-10, GBU-12 SERIES, GENERAL PURPOSE GUIDED, LASER TYPICAL

	GBU-10 SERIES	GBU-12 SERIES
WEIGHT (POUNDS)	2061	619
LENGTH (INCHES)	168	120
DIAMETER (INCHES)	18	11

when an AIM-9L fired from an A-10A successfully destroyed a drone helicopter at the White Sands Missile Range.

The usual defensive armament of the A/OA-10A is two AIM-9L/M Sidewinders mounted on LAU-114 launcher rails from the F-15 fighter. The LAU-114s are installed on an Air National Guard-developed dual rail adapter (DRA) on the left outboard wing station (#1), although it can also be mounted on the opposing station. Use of the DRA is optional, and a single Sidewinder can be carried without it. A-10s inadvertently fired three AIM-9s during Desert Storm.

An ECM pod is generally mounted on the wing station opposite the AIM-9s (usually #11). During Desert Storm, U.S.-based aircraft normally carried ALQ-119(V)-15 pods, while "shallow" ALQ-131s were carried on overseas-based aircraft. The ALQ-184(V)-1 and "deep" ALQ-131 pods can also be carried, although they do not appear to have been used during Desert Storm. In addition to ECM pods, A-10As carry ALE-40 chaff and flare countermeasures dispensers under their wingtips and at the back of the main landing gear sponsons. During Desert Storm, A/OA-10As expended 355,381 bundles of chaff and 108,654 flares in self-defense,

an average of over 40 bundles of chaff and 12 flares per sortie.

During Desert Storm, A-10As launched 5,013 AGM-65 Mavericks, over 90% of the Air Force total. Typically, a mix of $22,000 AGM-65A/B television and $141,000 AGM-65D IIR missiles were carried, although some $150,000 AGM-65G IIR versions were also used. The B and D versions were equipped with 125-pound shaped charge warheads for use against armor, while the G models were equipped with 300-pound kinetic penetrator warheads for use against high-value targets such as bunkers, locomotives, sheltered aircraft, and SAM sites. The

AGM-65Bs were used exclusively for daytime missions, and 1,692 were fired during the war. A total of 1,628 AGM-65Ds and 203 AGM-65Gs IIR missiles were fired during the daytime, with another 1,500 D-models fired at night. The success rates for all models was about 90%, with no appreciable differences in success rates between the two models. The AGM-65B was generally employed at ranges of 2–4 miles, while the AGM-65D was used at 4–8 miles. Interestingly, since the A-10 lacked any night vision equipment, pilots improvised by using their IIR Mavericks to hunt for targets in the dark. This proved to be remarkably successful.

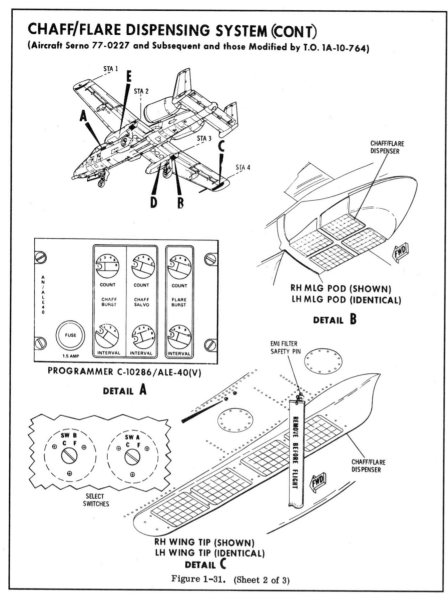

CHAFF/FLARE DISPENSING SYSTEM (CONT)
(Aircraft Serno 77-0227 and Subsequent and those Modified by T.O. 1A-10-764)

STA 1
STA 2
STA 3
STA 4
E
A
D
B
C

CHAFF/FLARE DISPENSER

RH MLG POD (SHOWN)
LH MLG POD (IDENTICAL)

DETAIL B

PROGRAMMER C-10286/ALE-40(V)

AN/ALE-40

COUNT CHAFF BURST
COUNT CHAFF SALVO
COUNT FLARE BURST

FUSE 1.5 AMP

INTERVAL INTERVAL INTERVAL

DETAIL A

SW B C F
SW A C F

SELECT SWITCHES

EMI FILTER SAFETY PIN

REMOVE BEFORE FLIGHT

CHAFF/FLARE DISPENSER

FWD

RH WING TIP (SHOWN)
LH WING TIP (IDENTICAL)

DETAIL C

Figure 1-31. (Sheet 2 of 3)

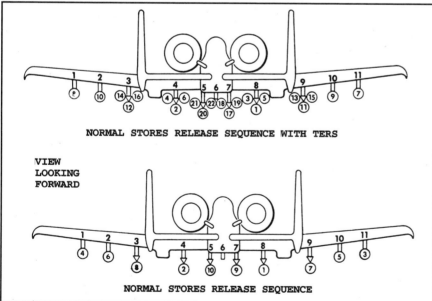

NORMAL STORES RELEASE SEQUENCE WITH TERS

VIEW LOOKING FORWARD

NORMAL STORES RELEASE SEQUENCE

A-10s after 77-0227 were equipped at the factory with AN/ALE-40 expendable countermeasure dispensers under the wingtips and at the rear of the landing gear sponsons. Earlier aircraft were all retrofitted in the field.
(U.S. Air Force)

Although pilots generally prefer the AGM-65D IIR Maverick, it does have several liabilities not generally seen during Desert Storm. High absolute humidity, fog, low ceilings, and precipitation can seriously degrade the operation of IR seekers, or even render them completely useless. Even the "ideal" desert conditions found during Desert Storm can present problems for IR seekers. Not every target is a good IR target; idle vehicles in the open sand, hot berms and bunker walls, camouflage netting, and diurnal effects often made target acquisition very difficult.

During the Gulf War the typical CAS mission for the A-10 included a radius of 475 miles with 1,174 rounds of combat mix ammunition, two AGM-65 Maverick missiles on LAU-117 rails on stations 3/9, an ALQ-131 ECM pod on station 11, and two AIM-9M Sidewinders on station 1. For the FACmission the OA-10 had a combat radius of 550 miles with 1,174 rounds of HEI ammunition, two LAU-10 rocket pods on stations 3/9, an ALQ-131 pod, and two Sidewinders.

This illustration shows the normal stores release sequence. The bottom is for parent-mounted weapons, while the top shows how it changes with the addition of triple ejection racks (TER). Even with TERs it is unusual to see three weapons mounted on a pylon. (U.S. Air Force)

MK 82 AND MK 84 LDGP BOMBS

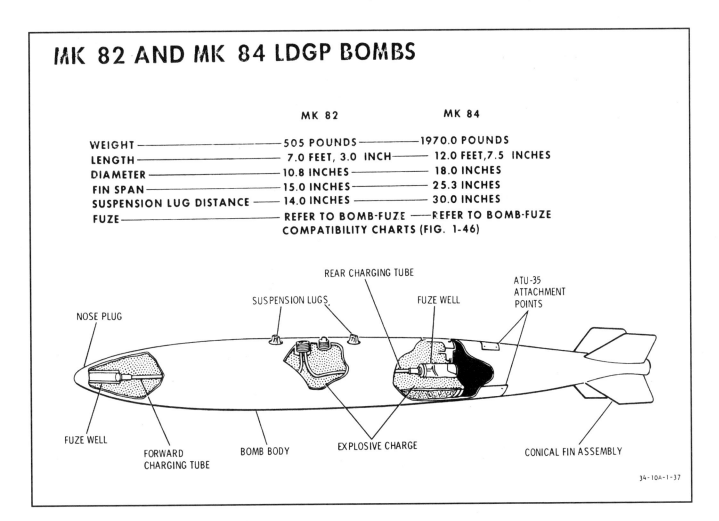

	MK 82	MK 84
WEIGHT	505 POUNDS	1970.0 POUNDS
LENGTH	7.0 FEET, 3.0 INCH	12.0 FEET, 7.5 INCHES
DIAMETER	10.8 INCHES	18.0 INCHES
FIN SPAN	15.0 INCHES	25.3 INCHES
SUSPENSION LUG DISTANCE	14.0 INCHES	30.0 INCHES
FUZE	REFER TO BOMB-FUZE COMPATIBILITY CHARTS (FIG. 1-46)	REFER TO BOMB-FUZE

NOSE PLUG · REAR CHARGING TUBE · SUSPENSION LUGS · FUZE WELL · ATU-35 ATTACHMENT POINTS · FUZE WELL · FORWARD CHARGING TUBE · BOMB BODY · EXPLOSIVE CHARGE · CONICAL FIN ASSEMBLY

34-10A-1-37

The standard "iron bomb" in the U.S. inventory is the Mk 82, which weighs 500 pounds. The Mk 84 is its big brother, weighing just under 2,000 pounds (but always referred to as a 2,000 pound bomb). Both bombs can be fitted with a set of "retarding fins" which slow the bomb down, allowing the aircraft more time to escape from extremely low level attacks. When fitted with the fins the bombs are known as Mk 82SE or Mk 84SE "Snakeyes". (U.S. Air Force)

MK 82 SNAKEYE 1 BOMB

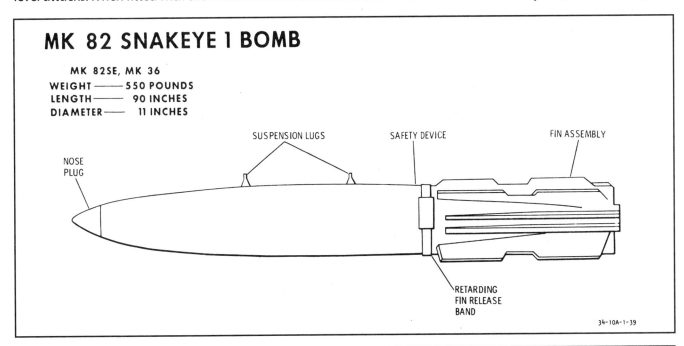

MK 82SE, MK 36
WEIGHT	550 POUNDS
LENGTH	90 INCHES
DIAMETER	11 INCHES

NOSE PLUG · SUSPENSION LUGS · SAFETY DEVICE · FIN ASSEMBLY · RETARDING FIN RELEASE BAND

34-10A-1-39

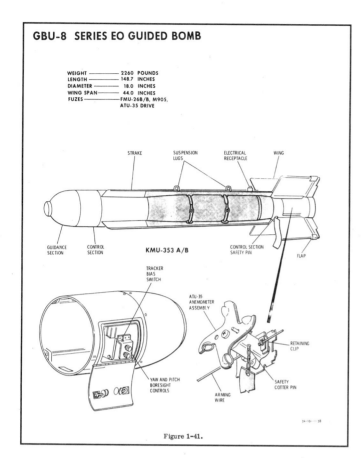

GBU-8 SERIES EO GUIDED BOMB

WEIGHT ———————— 2260 POUNDS
LENGTH ———————— 148.7 INCHES
DIAMETER ———————— 18.0 INCHES
WING SPAN ———————— 44.0 INCHES
FUZES ———————— FMU-26B/B, M905,
ATU-35 DRIVE

STRAKE
SUSPENSION LUGS
ELECTRICAL RECEPTACLE
WING
GUIDANCE SECTION
CONTROL SECTION
KMU-353 A/B
CONTROL SECTION SAFETY PIN
FLAP

TRACKER BIAS SWITCH
ATU-35 ANEMOMETER ASSEMBLY
RETAINING CLIP
YAW AND PITCH BORESIGHT CONTROLS
ARMING WIRE
SAFETY COTTER PIN

34-10-1-38

Figure 1-41.

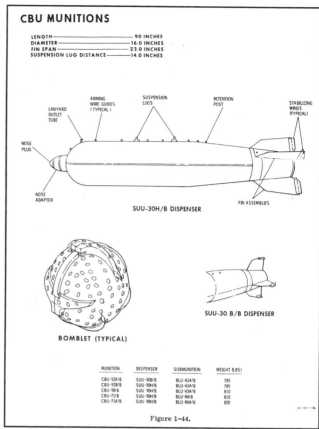

CBU MUNITIONS

LENGTH ———————— 90 INCHES
DIAMETER ———————— 16.0 INCHES
FIN SPAN ———————— 23.0 INCHES
SUSPENSION LUG DISTANCE ———————— 14.0 INCHES

LANYARD OUTLET TUBE
ARMING WIRE GUIDES (TYPICAL)
SUSPENSION LUGS
RETENTION POST
STABILIZING WINGS (TYPICAL)
NOSE PLUG
NOSE ADAPTER
SUU-30H/B DISPENSER
FIN ASSEMBLIES

BOMBLET (TYPICAL)

SUU-30 B/B DISPENSER

MUNITION	DISPENSER	SUBMUNITION	WEIGHT (LBS)
CBU-52A/B	SUU-30B/B	BLU-61A/B	785
CBU-52B/B	SUU-30H/B	BLU-61A/B	785
CBU-58/B	SUU-30H/B	BLU-63A/B	810
CBU-71/B	SUU-30H/B	BLU-86/B	810
CBU-71A/B	SUU-30H/B	BLU-86A/B	820

34-10A-1-86

Figure 1-44.

The A-10 could carry the GBU-8 electro-optically guided (basically a television) bomb, which was yet another kit that attached to a basic Mk 84 iron bomb. The CBU-52/58/71 cluster bombs can also be carried. (U.S. Air Force)

The Avenger 30mm cannon is made up of two large sub-assemblies. All spent shell casings are returned to the ammunition drum instead of being jettisoned overboard like some earlier cannon. This prevents the possibility of the large casings impacting the aircraft during firing, and also allows them to be reused if necessary. The feed mechanism is necessarily complex.

The other major subassembly is the barrels (inset on opposite page) and their associated drive mechanisms. The use of multiple barrels prevents any single barrel from overheating due to the high firing rate. (Mick Roth)

WARBIRD**TECH**
SERIES

AIM-9 Sidewinders are generally mounted on dual adapter rails, although they can be mounted on single rails directly under the pylon. (Ken Neubeck)

The second prototype A-10 was shown with a GAU-8/A cannon at the 1974 Edwards AFB air show. The size of the weapon relative to the aircraft (and it is a large aircraft) is readily apparent. (Mick Roth)

PLINKING TANKS

THE WARTHOG IN OPERATION DESERT STORM

The 23rd TFW(P) and 354th TFW(P) formed the 144-aircraft A/OA-10A force for Desert Shield/Storm, informally known as the "Fahd Squad." A total of five squadrons deployed, including two squadrons from Myrtle Beach AFB, one squadron from Joint Reserve base at New Orleans; one squadron from RAF Alconbury; and a squadron of OA-10A forward air controllers from Davis-Monthan AFB. The main operating location was located at the King Fahd International Airport, near Daharan in northeastern Saudi Arabia.

The A-10s made their wartime debut with the start of Operation Desert Storm on 15 January 1991. During Desert Storm, A/OA-10As flew 19,545.6 hours in 8,755 sorties (16.5% of the 53,000 sorties flown by the coalition), of which 7,445 delivered weapons (18% of the coalition's 41,000 strike sorties). Overall A-10 weapons system reliability during Desert Storm was 98.67% (this was the percentage of times weapons were successfully expended when desired). Targets listed as "confirmed kills" included 1,106 trucks, 987 tanks (25% of all

destroyed), 926 artillery pieces (again, about 25% of the war's total), 500 armored personnel carriers (30% of the total destroyed), 249 command vehicles, 112 military structures, 96 radars, 72 bunkers, 51 SCUD missile launchers, 50 anti-aircraft artillery batteries, 28 command posts, 11 FROG missile launchers, 10 parked fighter aircraft, 9 SAM sites, 8 fuel storage tanks, and 2 air-to-air helicopter kills.

On a single day during Desert Storm, two A-10s from the 76th TFS

The 23rd TFW is the famed "Flying Tigers" and flew their traditional sharkmouths during Operation Desert Storm. Although most of the crews were not altogether thrilled, the A-10 wore its standard European One camouflage in the desert. (Mick Roth Collection)

WARBIRDTECH
SERIES

Nose art indicates this aircraft has just returned from Operation Desert Storm. Air Force rules did not actually allow nose art, so it tended to be short-lived once back in the U.S. (David F. Brown via the Mick Roth Collection)

destroyed 23 Iraqi tanks. Capt. Eric "Fish" Salomonson and 1Lt. John "Karl" Marks each killed four tanks in Iraq, while Marks killed eight more in Kuwait and Salomonson killed seven.

Typical operations from King Fahd involved flying a sortie, landing at the King Khalid Military City (KKMC) FOL to re-arm, flying another sortie back to KKMC, then flying one last sortie to recover back at King Fahd. This resulted in about eight hours of flying time during a 12-hour duty day. However, if the missions involved SCUD hunting, the flying time would increase to about ten hours.

Many pilots and crews painted art on the inside of the boarding ladder door to make it less obvious and to not offend the Saudis (the door could be quickly closed when necessary). (Mick Roth Collection)

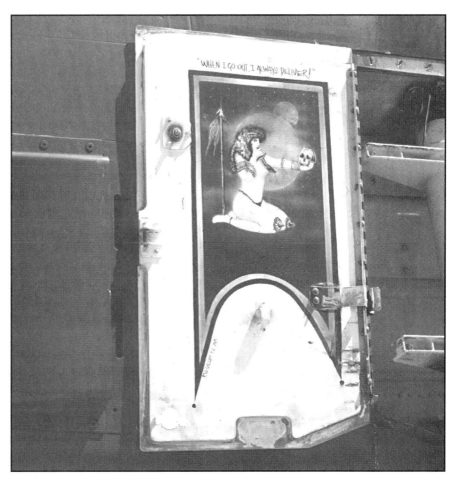

The infamous 384 holes in the tail of Colonel Sawyer's aircraft (80-0186). Photos similar to these have been published many times to illustrate the type of battle damage that the A-10 can absorb and still come home. This aircraft was returned to service within a few days. (MSgt Patrick J. McGee)

A second FOL, known as "Cajun West," was operated at Al Jouf, in far northern Saudi Arabia. Ten aircraft at a time were deployed there for five days before rotating back to King Fahd. Despite very primitive living conditions, the flying was relatively low threat and target rich. While their primary missions focused on SCUD hunting and support of special operations, other targets of opportunity soon presented themselves. These included a massive complex of munition storage bunkers and warehouses just north of the Baghdad-to-Amman highway in southwestern Iraq known as HOME DEPOT, and another, even larger, munitions storage area just south of the Euphrates River between Ramadi and the Syrian border named HICKSVILLE (after Capt. Al "Gator" Hicks, who discovered it). Early in the war, pilots would expend their remaining ordnance on one of these area targets on their way home from SCUD hunting. Later, as SCUDs became more difficult to find, pilots would expend most of their bombs on the area targets, reducing weight and drag so they could spend more time hunting for SCUDs with their Mavericks.

Each of the provisional wings also had a squadron designated for night combat. For the 354th TFW(P), this was the 355th TFS, which developed most of the night tactics used by A-10As during the

war. The squadron flew a dozen daytime missions against GCI sites during the first two days of the air war, and then flew exclusively at night for the rest of the war. After the first two weeks of the air war, the 74th TFS became the dedicated night squadron for the 23rd TFW(P).

The first A-10 battle damage during Desert Storm was caused by an aircraft flying through its own cannon shells. A single 30mm projectile

Not a good day. Captain Biley was piloting this A-10A (79-0181) when it was hit by an SA-3 during Operation Desert Storm. He managed to bring the aircraft back for a wheels-up landing, but the aircraft was a total write-off and was striped of all usable parts before being buried in the desert. (MSgt Patrick J. McGee)

Each squadron, and sometimes each crew chief, has a different way to string up the "remove before flight" tags on the side of the A-10. This aircraft only has a single "tag" with a rope connecting all the covers. Others have a tag on each cover, or something in between. (William D. Spidle via the Mick Roth Collection)

This photo is unusual in that both the Maverick (a training captive-carry round) and the PAVE PENNY pod are both painted dark. (P.D. Snow via the Mick Roth Collection)

pierced the primary outer skin of the wing leading edge, but luckily did not explode. The secondary structure received a minor dent. Ground personnel recovered the projectile, disarmed it, and presented it to the pilot as a souvenir. The pilot was unaware he had been hit. The aircraft was repaired and returned to service in less than nine hours. Other A-10s were not as fortunate. Since the A-10 frequently operated at low level in close support of ground forces, it tended to sustain more small arms and AAA damage than other aircraft types. One A-10 returned from a mission with 384 shrapnel and bullet holes. It was patched and returned to service within a few days. Two other aircraft had most of their tail sections shot away, while another lost most of its right wing. These aircraft were also repaired. Estimates were that as many as 70 of the 144 A-10s deployed received some type of damage, although many were undocumented cases of relatively minor problems.

The most celebrated demonstration of A-10 survivability was the return of an aircraft with most of its right wing missing, blown away by a shoulder-fired SAM which destroyed two of the three main

The A-10's relatively high wing makes it easier for the ground crews to work under it when loading weapons, almost all of which are carried and raised using the standard Air Force bomb truck shown beside the aircraft. This truck has a hydraulically actuated lift on it to raise the weapons into place. (Mick Roth)

wing spars, three adjacent ribs, all the stringers forward of the aft spar (the only one remaining), and more than 20 feet of skin on the upper wing surface. Normally, this aircraft would have been disassembled and returned to the Depot for repair, but in this case a new center wing section was shipped form the U.S. and installed by maintenance personnel in Saudi Arabia. The new wing section had previously been used for battle damage repair training at the Sacramento Air Logistics Center. The entire procedure only took four days to complete.

In another instance an A-10 returned with its right rudder inoperable due to heavy damage by shrapnel and the right elevator shot away. The left rudder and elevator had many holes but were still functioning. Yet another A-10 returned with no flight controls in the empennage at all, using only the engines and ailerons for control. At least one A-10, however, was considered too badly damaged to be repaired, and was stripped of all usable parts and buried in the desert.

The ALQ-131 ECM pod was generally carried by all aircraft operating in the Gulf War. In the United States and areas not actively engaged in combat the larger ALQ-119 can be carried, but this pod is less capable than the newer ALQ-131. (Michael Grove via the Mick Roth Collection)

"Fist". (Mick Roth)

"Wild Thing". (Ben Knowles via Mick Roth)

"Live and Let Die". (Ben Knowles via Mick Roth)

"Julie Ann". (Ben Knowles via Mick Roth)

"Missi Lynn". (Ben Knowles via Mick Roth)

"Mary Jane". (Ben Knowles via Mick Roth)

"Erin O". (Ben Knowles via Mick Roth)

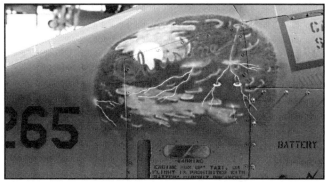

"Christine". (Ben Knowles via Mick Roth)

The size of the crewman gives an indication of how large an aircraft the A-10 really is. This explains the presence of ladders wherever the A-10 is stationed. The large access panels covering almost the entire fuselage allows crews easy access to all aircraft components without specialized tools. (Bruce Stewart via the Mick Roth Collection)

Surprisingly, the A-10 managed to score two air-to-air kills during Desert Storm, both made using the GAU-8/A cannon. The first was scored by Capt. Bob Swain from the 706th TFS against a BO-105 helicopter on 6 February 1991. The A-10 (77-0205) was later named "Chopper Popper" and is now displayed at the Air Force Armament Museum at Eglin AFB, Florida. The other was by Captain Todd "Shanghai" Sheehy from the 511th TFS, who shot down an Mi-8 on 15 February 1991.

Unfortunately, also on 15 February, two A-10As were shot down by infrared SAMs and another badly damaged. As part of the tactical changes implemented the next day to help prevent similar losses, gun use was suspended until 23 February, when the ground war began. In total, six A-10s were lost to infrared SAMs, and another 14 were substantially damaged, three by infrared SAMs and 11 by AAA.

The antennas on the side of the vertical stabilizer indicate this aircraft has been through the LASTE program (or is a testbed for it) but the lack of formation light strips means all the night vision updates have not been completed. The post-Gulf War modifications have greatly improved the A-10's effectiveness. (Mick Roth Collection)

NIGHT VISION

A two-seat configuration had been specified in the original A-X RFP, and both Northrop and Republic had included one in their proposals. The first preproduction aircraft was bailed back to Fairchild-Republic in April 1978 for conversion to the two-seat YA-10B, more commonly known as the Night/Adverse Weather (N/AW) A-10. Republic contributed $2 million of the $7.5 million development cost, with the rest funded by the Air Force. The two-seat modification took over a year to complete, mainly due to a low priority. The aircraft was delivered to Edwards AFB for flight tests, which began on 4 May 1979.

The N/AW was 2,000 pounds heavier than the normal single-seat version, and this was without increasing the titanium armor belt to protect the second crewman. The second seat was raised above the first, allowing the back-seat weapons systems officer relatively clear forward visibility. The second cockpit was essentially a duplicate of the front, except there was not a heads-up display. To compensate for the loss of directional control caused by adding the second seat, 20 inches was added to the top of the vertical stabilizers. A pod-mounted Westinghouse WX-50 ground-mapping radar was mounted on the left fuselage pylon (#5), with a Texas Instruments AAR-42 FLIR pod on the right fuselage pylon (#7). Had the A-10B been produced, the FLIR would have would have been integrated into the front of the right

main landing gear sponson, and only 6-8 inches would have been added to the vertical stabilizers. The aircraft was also fitted with a Litton LN-39 INS and dual Honeywell AN/APN-194 radar altimeters, and limited compatibility testing was accomplished with the AN/AVQ-26 PAVE TACK laser designator pod.

Unfortunately, the Air Force was not interested in the night-attack version, or a similar two-seat trainer version proposed by Republic. This was in spite of energetic marketing of the aircraft by Republic as a combat-ready trainer, pointing out huge cost savings to be made by removing the need for an instructor's chase aircraft on many A-10 conversion and tactical training sorties. The projected cost of pro-

The only two-seat A-10 built was the Night/Adverse Weather (N/AW) demonstrator. There has been some debate over whether this aircraft was ever officially designated YA-10B (there is no doubt production models would have been A-10Bs), and the records are not clear, although the aircraft currently has that designation painted in its data block. Note the increased height of the vertical stabilizer. Compare the amount the tail extends above the rudder to the photo on page 95. (Dave Begy via the Mick Roth Collection)

The two-seat prototype had side opening canopies instead of the upward opening unit of the single-seater. There were some pilot complaints about this and it is likely the canopy would have been changed on production models. (Fairchild-Republic)

duction A-10B conversions was $1.5 million; $500,000 for the airframe modifications, and a million for the avionics. Republic also marketed the A-10B as the basis for defense suppression, battlefield coordination, and interdictor versions. Unfortunately, all of these required the use of the LANTIRN system, which was slated for the higher priority F-15E and F-16C. The YA-10B was evaluated during 1979, but practical night attack with the A-10 did not become reality until 12 years later. The YA-10B is currently in storage at the Air Force Flight Test Center Museum, Edwards AFB, California.

Republic marketed the two-seat variant in the Pacific area as a maritime strike aircraft, carrying Harpoon or Exocet anti-ship missiles, but no orders were forthcoming. There have also been other stillborn A-10 variants. In

The modifications necessary to add the second seat were actually fairly minimal, even if it did take a long time for Republic to complete the work. The titanium "bathtub" was not extended to cover the second crewman on the prototype, although this would have been done in any production model. (Fairchild-Republic)

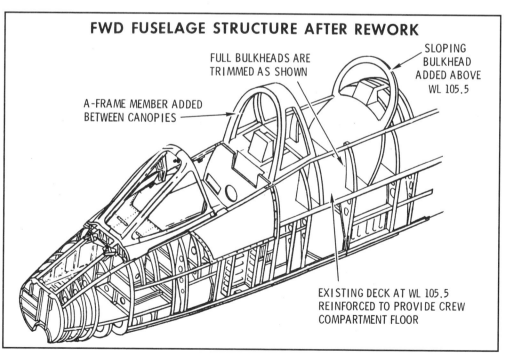

FWD FUSELAGE STRUCTURE AFTER REWORK

FULL BULKHEADS ARE TRIMMED AS SHOWN

SLOPING BULKHEAD ADDED ABOVE WL 105.5

A-FRAME MEMBER ADDED BETWEEN CANOPIES

EXISTING DECK AT WL 105.5 REINFORCED TO PROVIDE CREW COMPARTMENT FLOOR

A Texas Instruments AAR-42 forward looking infrared (FLIR) pod was carried on the right fuselage station but would have been integrated into the right main landing gear sponson if the N/AW A-10 had been ordered into production. A Westinghouse WX/50 ground mapping radar was carried in a white pod on the left fuselage station. (Mick Roth)

1976, Republic showed a model of the A-10 with long, slim nacelles housing non-afterburning versions of the J101 or RB.199 engines, trading endurance for higher speed. This would have given an increase of 50 knots in low level flight with weapons, but was not sufficient to overcome the prejudices of the intended customers, who regarded a 450-knot attack aircraft as obsolete, regardless of whether the U.S. Air Force was flying them or not.

All of this meant that the A-10 did not possess a night attack capability when it was deployed to the Gulf in 1991, and the lack of a FLIR hindered initial night practice during Operation Desert Shield. However, pilots in the Gulf quickly realized that the AGM-65D IIR Maverick missile could be used as a "poor man's FLIR," although this went against the accepted tactical doctrine taught by the Fighter Weapons School. Better than nothing, the

Maverick nevertheless makes a fairly ineffective FLIR since its widest field of view is 3°, while the narrow field of view is only 1.5°. For example, from an ingress altitude of 7,000 feet and a range of 7 miles, the "view" provided by the Maverick is 2.3 miles long by 2,200 feet wide. This is a fairly narrow corridor to try and find a target in. The use of an IIR Maverick as a means of identifying targets has been generally accepted within the A-10 community now, and tactics have been developed and published based mainly on the results of the two night-fighting A-10 squadrons in Desert Storm.

The N/AW aircraft was modified from the first DT&E aircraft (73-1664) using Republic corporate funds with some Air Force funding. Total cost of the modification was approximately $500,000 for the airframe and another $1,000,000 for the adverse weather avionics. Although the aircraft proved very capable, the Air Force was already committed to other aircraft and no orders were forthcoming. (Cradle of Aviation Museum via Ken Neubeck)

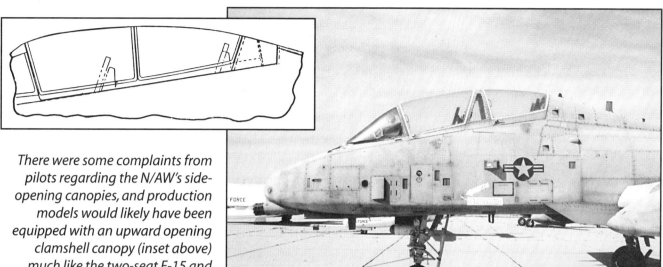

There were some complaints from pilots regarding the N/AW's side-opening canopies, and production models would likely have been equipped with an upward opening clamshell canopy (inset above) much like the two-seat F-15 and F-16 fighters use.
(Dennis R. Jenkins)

During the late 1980s the low-altitude safety and targeting enhancement (LASTE) program was initiated to install several high-technology improvements into the rather basic A-10 avionics suite. The first, generally called a ground collision avoidance system (GCAS), was a radar altimeter coupled with a voice warning system to improve the pilot's situational awareness at low altitude. If the pilot descends beneath a preselected altitude (usually 90 feet AGL), or at too steep an angle to recover, the system warns him in time to avoid hitting the ground. An even greater improvement was the installation of the same weapons delivery computer used by the F-16. Even though the A-10 lacks the radar of the F-16, the computer dramatically improved bombing accuracy. In addition to displaying a continuously computed impact point (CCIP) bombing solution on the head-up display (HUD), it also provided a projection of the bullet trajectory to the A-10 pilots for the first time. An air-to-air gun sight, improvement to the HUD symbology, and a software support system for future enhancements were also

The N/AW originally had vertical stabilizers that were approximately 20 inches higher than normal, although the rudders remained their original size. At some point during the test program, although exactly when could not be determined, about 12 inches were removed from the verticals. Compare this photo to the ones on page 39 and page 94.
(Dennis R. Jenkins)

added as part of LASTE. But perhaps the most popular improvement was the addition of an enhanced attitude control (EAC) system, better known as an autopilot—the A-10 being perhaps the last American combat aircraft to acquire one.

Fleet modification to the LASTE standard did not begin in earnest until after Desert Storm in mid-1991. While most of the LASTE modifications were installed at the Sacramento Air Logistics Depot, some aircraft were modified at their overseas bases. Competing against other fighters with the help of these improvements for the first time in the 1991 Gunsmoke bombing competition, the 175th Tactical Fighter Group (ANG) from Balti-

This A-10 has received all the recent modifications. The formation light strips on the forward fuselage, wingtips, and vertical stabilizers are part of the night vision package. (Don Logan)

more, Maryland, won the semi-annual contest. Unfortunately, the LASTE equipment has proven to be less than ideally reliable.

Despite the success of the A-10 in Desert Storm, the lack of night vision goggles (NVG) and compatible cockpit lighting severely limited the night deployment capabilities. The original cockpit lighting operated with wavelengths, (both visible and near infrared) that rendered NVGs unusable. A modification was developed for the installation of vastly improved cockpit lighting that made the A-10 compatible with NVGs, and exterior strip lighting was added to improve safety during night formation flying. Direction for the modifications came from Headquarters Air Combat Command in the form of a Combat Mission Need Statement, validated by the Chief of Staff of the Air Force in June 1993.

The need for night vision equipment was considered an urgently needed combat capability, and a requirement was issued for the acquisition, modification, and logistics support to modify 100 aircraft by October 1994, and 150 more by October 1995. The remainder of the operational fleet was due for completion in October 1996. However, due to insufficient funding and production lead time this timetable could not be met. The revised schedule was a "do the best you can" agreement, with the goal of 250 aircraft modified by October 1995. A sole source contract was awarded to Grumman Aerospace in March 1994 and the modifications were performed in the field at the A-10 operating sites. Because Air Combat Command expressed the need for all A-10 aircraft to be modified with the night vision package, a follow-on contract was awarded to Grumman that resulted in the entire operational A/OA-10 fleet being modified by the end of 1997.

In 1996 the Air Force conducted an in-depth review of the reliability and availability of the A/OA-10A. Availability is a measure of the time an aircraft is in mission capable (partially or full) status. It is a function of how often an item fails, how long it takes to repair, and the supply of spares. The top ten items affecting availability contained some surprises. The TF34 engines were the most unreliable component on the aircraft, followed by the GAU-8, the fuel tanks, various controls in the cockpit, the HUD and guidance computer, the canopy, and the main landing gear. Currently, mainly due to funding limitations, the only modification being done on the TF34 engine is replacing the engine gearbox bearings with better ones and improving the lubrication. Most of the other items are not being addressed due to funding constraints and the low priority afforded the A-10.

Also during this review it was estimated that for FY97 the cost of flying the A-10A was $1,504 per hour. This amount includes consumable supplies, depot maintenance (which is primarily engine overhaul costs), depot level repair costs, and

aviation fuel. It did not include the pilot's salary, nor amortizing the cost of acquiring and sustaining the aircraft.

During the early 1990s one of the highest failure items was the inertial navigation system, which also cost $18,000 per unit. Luckily, technology has vastly improved in this area, and the A-10 fleet is receiving new INS units integrated with the global positioning satellite (GPS) system. This should improve the availability of the aircraft, as well as provide better navigational data to the pilot and shorten the amount of time necessary to launch a support mission (aligning the INS usually takes time at a known location on the airfield—GPS removes this limitation). The GPS information is displayed on the TV display unit used for the Maverick missile. This, however, presents another problem. The TV unit itself has proven to be somewhat unreliable, and now it is used all the time instead of the

10% of the mission required for Maverick launches. The Air Force is investigating replacing the TV monitor with a multifunction display similar to those used on the F-16 and other modern fighters.

With the almost incomprehensible state of flux in the American military, it is difficult to predict how much longer the A-10 will continue to serve. There are 180 aircraft currently in flyable storage in AMARC at Davis-Monthan. The Air Force seems to be keeping the remaining aircraft operational more because the Army wants them to rather than for any real appreciation of the aircraft's abilities.

When the U.S. was looking at phasing out the A-10 during the early 1990s, several other countries expressed interest in obtaining them. During mid-1993 there was a high probability that Turkey would buy 50 aircraft for approximately $167 million until the State Depart-

ment objected to exporting the DU ammunition used in the GAU-8/A. There was also a cost issue. The $167 million was for the basic A-10A configuration, without the LASTE upgrades, support, or training. By the time all the ancillary costs were factored in, Turkey could not afford the aircraft and opted for additional F-4s. Israel, Korea, and Egypt also expressed interest, but in the end no aircraft were released to any foreign operator.

During the early 1990s AeroTech Ltd. developed a concept for using retired A-10s as the next-generation of fire-fighting airtankers. Appropriately, this design was called the "Firehog". In order to underscore the potential of the A-10 to replace the current generation of airtankers, AeroTech arranged for two military A-10s to fly a demonstration for fire fighters at Marine Corps Air Station El Toro, California, on 18 September 1997. The Firehog would have been mod-

A-10s from the 917th Wing rotate into Aviano, Italy, as part of the U.N. mission in Bosnia. This aircraft is carrying a Maverick, target marking rockets, and a deep ALQ-131 ECM pod under the left wing. The formation light strips means this aircraft has received the night vision modifications. (917th WG / PA via Don Logan)

Since no two-seat A-10 was ever procured, instructor pilots "shadow" their students in another A-10 for the first few flights.(Don Logan)

ified with a large belly tank under the wing/fuselage area to carry fire retardant. Unlike amphibious tankers or helicopters, the Firehog would have to return to a fixed base to be refilled after every drop, but the A-10's excellent short-field performance and quiet operations lessens the impact from this handicap. This concept made a great deal of sense when it was expected that the A-10 would be retired by the end of 1991. However, since the Air Force has decided to keep the A-10 in active service for the foreseeable future, it is unlikely that the Air Force would be willing to release any of the 180 aircraft currently in flyable storage.

On 8 January 1998 Lockheed Martin Federal Systems in Owego, New York, was selected by the Air Force to become the new "prime" contractor for the A/OA-10A. This is somewhat unique in the history of American military aircraft. Usually the contractor that originally designs and builds the aircraft continues to perform sustaining engineering for modifications, etc. for the life of the aircraft. In this case, the original prime contractor, Fairchild-Republic, ceased to exist as an aircraft manufacturer. For a time Grumman, a fellow New York aerospace company, took on the role as the sustainer of the A-10. However, Grumman fell on hard times and later merged with Northrop, largely getting out of the aircraft business. The Air Force performed the sustaining function in-house for a period, but in the end decided it wanted a contractor to do it. The nine year, $488 million contract calls for Lockheed Martin to develop and integrate modifications, including software and support infrastructure, and to be the primary provider of sustaining engineering. Lockheed Martin has already provided the software and hardware required for the A-10 LASTE program.

This 81st FS A-10 from Spangdalem AB was photographed at Aviano during August 1996 in support of the U.N. forces in Bosnia. Many A-10 units have supported this activity on a rotational basis. (Alec Fushi via Don Logan)

SIGNIFICANT DATES

1947
The "A – Attack" category is abolished from the Air Force designation system

1961
The U.S. Army evaluates procuring a dedicated Close Air Support aircraft

LATE 1961
The first "COIN' detachment arrive in Vietnam

1964
The U.S. Army begins development of the Aerial Fire Support System (AFSS)—the AH-56A Cheyenne

6 MARCH 1967
Initial conceptual A-X RFPs released to 21 aerospace companies

2 MAY 1967
A-X engineering support contracts issued to General Dynamics, McDonnell, and Northrop

1967
Israeli Defense Forces demonstrate effective tank killing using their Dassault Mysteres

12 MAY 1970
Competitive prototype RFPs released to 12 aerospace companies

10 AUGUST 1970
Responses received from Boeing-Vertol, Cessna, Fairchild-Republic, Lockheed, and Northrop

18 DECEMBER 1970
Fairchild-Republic and Northrop selected to build 2 A-X prototypes each

15 JANUARY 1973
General Electric and Philco-Ford begin side-by-side firing trials of new 30mm cannon

21 JUNE 1973
General Electric selected to develop the GAU-8/A 30mm cannon

FEBRUARY 1971
The Department of Defense begins an extensive study of Close Air Support concepts and options

EARLY 1971
U.S. Air Force conducts the TAC-85 study of tactical air support, including the CAS mission

LATE 1971
Both TAC-85 and the DoD study vindicate the A-X concept

10 MAY 1972
The first YA-10 makes its first flight at Edwards AFB

30 MAY 1972
The first YA-9 makes its first flight at Edwards AFB

24 OCTOBER 1972
The A-10 Joint Task Force begins evaluating the two A-X competitors

18 JANUARY 1973
Fairchild-Republic declared the winner of the A-X competition. Ten YA-10A DT&E aircraft ordered

JULY 1973
Four of the ten DT&E aircraft cancelled by Congress when the Air Force does not conduct a fly-off between the A-10 and a modified A-7

15 APRIL 1974
The Air Force finally begins the A-10 versus A-7 fly-off

JUNE 1974
The A-10 is declared the winner of the fly-off

MID-1974
Production funding for 52 A-10As released by the Air Force

JULY 1974
The GAU-8/A is certified for flight in the A-10

SEPTEMBER 1974
The first YA-10 prototype is retrofitted with the GAU-8 cannon

15 FEBRUARY 1975
The first YA-10A DT&E aircraft makes its first flight at Edwards AFB

15 APRIL 1975
The first YA-10 prototype is retired

26 APRIL 1975
The second YA-10A DT&E aircraft becomes the first A-10 to fly from Republic's facilities in New York

10 OCTOBER 1975
The first production A-10A makes its maiden flight

3 JUNE 1977
Sam Nelson is killed when his A-10A crashes at the Paris Air Show

27 OCTOBER 1977
The first YA-10 is installed on a tower on the Rome Laboratory test range

3 APRIL 1978
The 100th A-10A is completed and the aircraft is officially christened "Thunderbolt II"

JANUARY 1979
The first A-10As are delivered to the 81st TFW in Europe; deliveries to the AFRES and ANG follow

DECEMBER 1981
Integration of the AIM-9 Sidewinder begins, giving the A-10 a limited defensive capability

JANUARY 1991
A-10As participate in Operation Desert Storm, devastating the Iraqi tank force during 8,755 sorties

8 JANUARY 1998
Lockheed Martin in Owego New York becomes the new "prime contractor" for the A-10

A-10 Units and Tailcodes

Operators of the Warthog

Tailcode	Unit and Location
AD	3246th Test Wing, Eglin AFB, Florida
AK	343rd Wing, Eielson AFB, Alaska
AK	354th FW, Eielson AFB, Alaska
AR	10th TFW, RAF Alconbury, England
BC	110th FG (ANG), William K. Kellogg Airport, Michigan
BD	917th TFG/TFW/Wing (AFRES), Barksdale AFB, Louisiana
CT	103rd FG (ANG), Bradley ANGB, Connecticut
DM	355th TFW/FW/WG, Davis-Monthan AFB, Arizona
ED	6510th Test Wing, Edwards AFB, California
ED	412th Test Wing, Edwards AFB, California
EL	23rd TFW, England AFB, Louisiana
ET	3246th Test Wing, Eglin AFB, Florida
FT	23rd WG, Pope AFB, North Carolina
ID	190th FS / 124th WG (ANG), Gowne Field, Boise, Idaho
IN	424th TFW (AFRES), Grissom AFB, Indiana
IN	930th TFG/OG (AFRES), Grissom AFB, Indiana
KC	442nd TFG/TFW/FW (AFRES), Whiteman AFB, Missouri
MB	354th TFW/FW, Myrtle Beach, South Carolina
MA	104th FG (ANG), Barnes ANGB, Massachusetts
MD	175th FG (ANG), Warfield ANGB, Maryland
MY	347th WG, Moody AFB, Georgia
NF	602nd ACW, Davis-Monthan AFB, Arizona
NO	706th TFS / 926th TFG (AFRES), JRB New Orleans, Louisiana
NY	174th TFW (ANG), Hancock Field, New York
OS	51st TFW/FW, Osan AB, Korea
OT	4443rd Test and Evaluation Group, Eglin AFB, Florida
OT	57th Test Group, Nellis AFB, Nevada
PA	111th FG (ANG), Willow Grove ARB, Pennsylvania
SF	507th ACW, Shaw AFB, South Carolina
SM	2874th Test Squadron, McClellan AFB, California
SM	337th Test Squadron, McClellan AFB, California
SP	52nd FW, Spangdhalem AB, Germany
SU	51st TFW, Suwon AB, Korea
SW	363rd FW, Shaw AFB, South Carolina
SW	20th FW, Shaw AFB, South Carolina
TC	354th FS, McChord AFB, Washington
WA	57th FWW/TTW/WG, Nellis AFB, Nevada
WI	128th TFW/FW (ANG), Truax ANGB, Wisconsin
WR	81st TFW, RAF Bentwaters/RAF Woodbridge, England